THE HEAD OF YEAR'S HANDBOOK

driving student
well-being and
engagement

THE HEAD OF YEAR'S HANDBOOK

driving student
well-being and
engagement

Michael Power

Routledge
Taylor & Francis Group

LONDON AND NEW YORK

First published in 2020 by Critical Publishing Ltd

Published 2025 by Routledge
4 Park Square, Milton Park, Abingdon, Oxon OX14 4RN
605 Third Avenue, New York, NY 10017

Routledge is an imprint of the Taylor & Francis Group, an informa business

British Library Cataloguing in Publication Data
A CIP record for this book is available from the British Library

ISBN: 9781913063214 (pbk)
ISBN: 9781041057505 (ebk)

The right of Michael Power to be identified as the Author of this work has been asserted by him in accordance with the Copyright, Design and Patents Act 1988.

Portrait illustration by Élisabeth Eudes-Pascal represented by GCI

Cover and text design by Out of House Limited

DOI: 10.4324/9781041057505

DEDICATION

To my wife Lucy and daughter Emily, for supporting me through writing this book and reminding me to look after my own well-being as I advise others to do the same.

To all the students and adults I have had the opportunity to lead or be led by, thank you for being the inspiration and foundation for *The Head of Year's Handbook*.

CONTENTS

MEET THE AUTHOR

MICHAEL POWER

I originally qualified as a youth worker and managed youth work provision across multiple youth centres for a local authority. I then qualified as a teacher and have worked in a small rural school in North Wales, a large Church of England school in Cheshire and an academy converter in Greater Manchester that was in special measures. I have experienced a wealth of issues in the role of head of year alongside engaging in my own original research for a Master's degree in educational practice. This collaboration between academic research and lived experience across a variety of settings provides a unique perspective for understanding the head of year role.

PREFACE

Being a head of year is by far one of the most rewarding, yet challenging, roles within secondary education. I have been privileged enough to hold this position for a number of years and much of my own experience has influenced what you will read in the pages of this book.

Before becoming a head of year I was a youth worker. I led youth clubs for a local authority and was able to see first-hand the benefits of pastoral work with students. I was able to experience dealing with a number of issues which I would later revisit as a head of year, such as bereavement, anti-social behaviour in the community and students who have found themselves no longer in education, employment or training. I am almost certain that if I had not spent time honing the skills of building positive relationships and discussing issues with students in an informal setting, the transition from classroom teacher to head of year would have been more difficult.

I have seen a number of new heads of year come to the role not knowing what to expect or indeed what their students will expect of them. Alongside this, for many teaching heads of year, this is the first time they have been involved in day-to-day pastoral work beyond their own classrooms. While there is much reading around how to lead an academic department within a school there is little that focuses on pastoral leadership, and where these books do exist they often avoid focusing on the dual role of a teacher and head of year. You are primarily a teacher. However, you not only have to teach your students, you need to be at the forefront of dealing with the behaviour, attendance, progress and pastoral needs of the students in your year group. It is indeed a juggling act.

Although it would be impossible to provide a complete one-stop shop for everything a head of year will face, I hope what I have created here provides you with a flavour of the issues you will come up against and a starting point for creating your own plan of action.

Managing this juggling act will allow you to support your students in ways that a classroom teacher cannot, and in doing so you will have influence over lives in ways others simply cannot imagine. You are a leader within your school for both students and colleagues because of the huge changes you will support others through or can bring about in order to support those around you. Despite this leadership role it is often the case that heads of year are ill-prepared for their role as a leader and can struggle to make sense of their position as a middle leader within a school.

The pastoral work of schools is, in my opinion, the most important element of what a school has to offer. My research as a Master's student and now as a doctoral student has highlighted that the impact teaching has on a student's outcomes and future life chances is far less than the impact of the pastoral care they are given. Despite this fact, the majority of schools will not give the same status to a head of year as they do to a head of department, which means it truly is a vocation within a vocation.

At a time where there is increasing pressure upon schools to provide additional pastoral care with tighter budgets, heads of year find themselves on the front line of dealing with an increasing number of issues with fewer support services to turn to. This can feel like an impossible task, but with every small breakthrough you will have made a real difference to the lives of your students. This is why I am adamant that being a head of year is one of the most rewarding roles within a modern secondary school.

Although the importance of your role as a head of year is clear, it is vital that you do not allow it to become all-consuming. When you are exhausted, you cannot be at your best. Remember to use your team, pass on the skills of good pastoral care and allow yourself the time to reflect on your work.

I find that at its simplest, the role of a head of year falls into two categories, well-being and engagement. If you can develop an understanding of what it means to drive progress in these two areas you will become a great head of year.

Michael Power, 2020

INTRODUCTION

How to use this book

The Head of Year's Handbook has been designed as a practical companion to one of the most rewarding yet challenging roles within a school. It looks in depth at what a head of year does on a day-to-day basis, the challenges you will face, and provides strategies and ideas to improve student outcomes and develop your own leadership ability.

The book is suitable for those just starting out as a head of year or those who have been in the role for a number of years and need some inspiration when facing new challenges. The role of head of year is ever-changing and must respond to issues facing both students and society as a whole. This book provides the inspiration needed to tackle the challenges and develops your own leadership ability in the process, with case studies and reflection points.

Although the book can be read cover to cover, it is also possible to dip in and out of the book at key points, depending on the challenges you are facing at any given moment. For example, if you are about to inherit a new tutor team you might look at Chapter 17 on managing your team, or if you are struggling to improve your year group's attendance you might look at Chapter 6 on driving attendance.

Chapter features

Within each chapter, there are a number of common features designed to help you get to grips with the content and key concepts.

CASE STUDY

Each chapter includes a case study that demonstrates some of the skills and scenarios that are discussed within that chapter. These case studies are based on real-life experiences of current and previous heads of year and reflect how what you are reading about could play out in reality.

Although each case study focuses on the content of each chapter, as a head of year what you face will rarely fit within just one of the chapters in this book and often multiple issues will present themselves at once. You should use the case studies to build up an overall picture of what life of a head of year can look like.

REFLECTIONS

Towards the end of each chapter are a number of reflection points. These are designed to guide your thinking and help you to implement each section's learning in your own practice. You might find it useful to write your answers and reflections into a journal, or you can simply think about the answers as you read through the pages.

REFERENCES

At the very end of each chapter is a reference list. These not only provide you with links to support the chapter, but include a wide range of additional reading should you wish to delve deeper into a particular area of work.

A focus on well-being and engagement

Well-being and engagement are the threads that run through this book and which should flow through all of your work as a head of year. Well-being can have a profound impact on students throughout their school lives, from a one-off incident to more long-term and complex mental health concerns. Schools need to respond to the well-being needs of their students through development of good pastoral care, tackling bullying issues and raising the aspirations of each year group.

Rather than simply focusing on behaviour, you should be concentrating on student engagement. This allows you as the head of year to respond more appropriately to the needs of your students and also means that you deal with underlying problems which could become more deep-seated and difficult to work with.

Much of the work a head of year will do around promoting engagement and tackling behaviour will be to set the standard, model it and foster an environment that promotes engagement from your year group. There will always be times when students choose not to engage in their education, and at times there will be no underlying cause that you can discern. Students are unpredictable in their nature. It is your job to provide the consistency they need to make sense of the learning environment.

Ultimately I believe that where the focus is kept on well-being and engagement, not only can any challenges that you face in your role be resolved, but a culture of dealing with underlying issues can be developed which will bring about long-term positive change for your students.

1. GREAT YEAR LEADERSHIP

Being a great head of year

Being a head of year is one of the most rewarding yet challenging roles within education. You are at the forefront of dealing with parents, staff and the students themselves. The role has many demands that can change between settings but the qualities that make you a great head of year are consistent.

You are trusted with leading a team of dedicated staff in developing your year group. Your vision for the future of your cohort will determine how they experience school and will determine whether this is a positive or negative experience (Buck, 2017). Heads of year are some of the most memorable people in a child's life and are role models of how to work with other people and deal with a plethora of difficult situations.

With such a huge and influential task at hand, the need to be truly great as a head of year should be at the forefront of any head of year's mind. It should form the foundations of any of the work you complete as a head of year and provide a bedrock from which your skills can develop and provide the best support, encouragement and leadership for your students.

At the heart of being a great head of year is an ability to build positive relationships with pupils, staff and other stakeholders. These relationships will allow you to provide guidance, set your vision and provide challenge when necessary. Building up positive relationships is more than smiling at everybody and saying hello; much of your work as a head of year will be building up key relationships through listening to the worries of others, giving people your time and showing that you care about their issues. Ultimately, it comes down to understanding people and being empathetic to their fears. Over time, this will lead colleagues to trust you and will allow you to become more than just a managerial figure. For your students, establishing a good relationship is central to tackling issues around behaviour and also being able to support your students in times of need (Scarlett et al, 2008).

Combining your ability to build positive relationships with the four key qualities of a great head of year outlined below will ensure your practice is as effective as it can be. You will be able to lead your year group and staff team, and eventually move on to lead on issues across the whole school.

Qualities of a great head of year

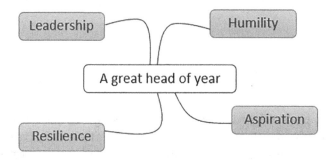

Figure 1.1 Qualities of a great head of year

LEADERSHIP

Being a head of year is first and foremost a leadership role. Unlike other leadership roles, a whole cohort of students will be looking to you for guidance on any number of issues. As a truly great head of year you are tasked with managing your team of tutors and associated staff in their support of your year group to achieve their best while at school.

In leading your team you will not only set and monitor tasks but also create an identity and clear vision for improvement and be responsible for ensuring everybody in the team plays their part in achieving your vision (Rowland, 2015).

In leading your students you will need to set high expectations to create a purposeful learning experience, but you will also be the person that students turn to in their times of need. You will deal with the very intense highs of being of secondary school age while also trying to mitigate the inevitable lows that occur in every student's life.

Your task as a leader is to balance the needs of the two groups for whom you are responsible, the students and the staff. You must provide unwavering support for both groups while making it clear that both are accountable to you as their leader.

ASPIRATION

Your aspirations as a head of year are what drive much of the work your team will do and ultimately provide the framework required by the students to overcome barriers in their lives. Aspiration motivates you to work harder and will also inspire those you lead to work harder, to achieve your shared goals and vision (Brown, 2018).

Your vision sets a clear benchmark that will be used to judge your success as a head of year. For many, this could lead to expectations being lowered; however, as a great head of year you need to push beyond what is easily achievable and look towards what can make your year group's experience of school even better. Your school will no doubt have targets for you to meet concerning progress, behaviour and attendance, but there is nothing to stop you going further and being better. This aspiration to do better is what sets a great head of year apart.

Your aspirations as a head of year should move beyond those in targets and look to the wider lives and skill sets of your year group. In your position you are able to affect a wider range of factors in a student's life, which will impact upon them long after they have left your care. A truly aspirational head of year will look to both how they can achieve their targets and how they can have a positive impact upon their students' futures. Studies have demonstrated that good leadership has a positive effect on the psychological well-being of your students (Nielsen et al, 2008), so getting leadership right is vitally important if you are to drive student well-being.

RESILIENCE

Be under no illusion, being a head of year can be tough. As a great head of year, you have set yourself aspirational targets and at times you will feel as though they are unachievable. You will need to be able to push on when times are tough and you feel like no progress is being made. The hard truth of being a head of year is that so much of what goes on in school is beyond your control, and you may feel that you are left picking up the pieces.

Ultimately, children are unpredictable. How they respond to any number of issues could set you and your vision back or force you to spend more time on crisis management or dealing with low-level issues that are a distraction from your core business and what you want to achieve. This will happen a lot. As a resilient head of year you will need to come to terms with never finishing your to-do list and always being side-tracked by an unforeseen circumstance (Morrish, 2016). The path to success is marred, and changes in direction of the school's leadership can create conflict between your ethos and theirs.

It is a well-held belief that working in a pastoral role in schools is one of the most challenging; when you finally gain control of one situation another will arise and you will feel like nothing is improving. Stay true to your vision and take time to have an overview of your year group. This way you can see exactly what progress is being made and spot issues on the horizon. Being prepared for new issues and having a strategy for your team to stick to will help you to overcome the challenges of leadership and remain resilient in a very challenging role.

HUMILITY

As a head of year you hold a highly privileged role within the lives of countless numbers of children and staff. In this scenario it is easy to see why some would start to see themselves as the front man in a band or as a professional athlete with their supporting team in tow. Of course this view of things can quickly create issues for a head of year.

You will get things wrong so it is important not to dwell on these instances but be willing to hold your hands up and accept that mistakes have been made. Apologise where necessary but then learn from these mistakes and demonstrate true leadership ability. When things are going well, a great head of year must still act with humility; the unpredictable nature of the job means you will often need to seek the support of others in the not so distant future.

It is important that you remember the unique contributions each member of your team makes and take pride in celebrating their success and the successes of your students above your own. Being a great head of year is not a one-person show but a careful collaboration of a whole team of people. Likewise, you will come face to face with issues facing students in their lives which to you might appear to be trivial. It is important to really understand how life experiences are affecting your students and be able to admit that you don't have all of the answers – sometimes you will need to get help to best support your students.

Case study

QUALITIES IN ACTION

Tom was a head of year at a large secondary academy in Birmingham. He arrived at school early to prepare for a tutor briefing where he would introduce his latest strategy to improve attendance for his year group. This involved tutors completing interviews with students after every absence and creating an action plan to avoid future absences.

Tom shared his idea with his tutor team. He started by showing student attainment compared with attendance, and highlighted to the team the clear trend that students achieve less when their attendance drops below 96 per cent. He then explained how tutors would need to complete the new 'return to school' interviews every day. The initial response from Tom's tutor team was one of scepticism. The tutors did not believe that this would help improve attendance, but rather would increase their workload. One tutor was very vocal at the meeting. They stated that Tom was being unrealistic and they also suggested that the new idea would be detrimental to the relationship between the students and their tutors.

Tom agreed with his team that he would take their feedback on board. He asked the team to bring their own suggestions on how to improve attendance to their next meeting. At the end of the meeting, Tom spoke to the vocal member of staff and explained that raising attendance needed to be a priority if the team were going to help students to make progress. Both agreed that attendance should be a focus and the member of staff agreed to come with ideas to the next meeting.

In this short case study, Tom led his team in a briefing. It is clear that Tom had aspirations to improve the attendance of his year group. He worked to help others understand his vision by showing what impact low attendance can have on outcomes for students. He demonstrated humility by allowing the team to voice concerns and offering to adjust his plan. He knows he doesn't have all the answers. Tom had spent time preparing for this meeting but was able to continue working towards his goals, even when the team members did not agree with his proposed solution, showing clear resilience. The whole case study demonstrates how the key qualities of a great head of year come together even in the smallest of instances. Ultimately the vocal member of staff was concerned about not only their own workload but the impact this could have on the students, which should be at the forefront when making any decisions for your year group.

Summary

These truly great qualities provide an insight into what can make you a great head of year. The ability to lead a group of students and staff towards a common set of goals is a challenge and there will be times when even the greatest head of year finds it difficult to plot a course forward. What you must remember as a great head of year is that you have the power to affect a great deal of change for your students and your staff team. You have the ability to make people's time at school the most memorable years of their lives. Likewise, your actions can have wide-reaching consequences, meaning the pressure to get it right is ever-present.

Being a great head of year involves understanding the unique needs of your students within your unique context, remaining optimistic about the future for your students and leading a team with skilful tenacity, while celebrating the success of every member who contributes to your success. As a head of year, you are the captain of a ship; without all of the other members of the team you cannot sail. Without you, the ship would be without direction and struggle to adapt to an ever-changing environment.

❖ Reflections

1. What do you think makes you a great head of year?

2. What are your key areas for development as a head of year?

3. How would you respond if a member of your team was not on board with your idea?

4. What are your aspirations as a great head of year? How will these support the well-being and development of your students?

5. How do you recognise the contributions of your team? What else could you do?

6. How do you recognise the achievements of your students? What more could you do?

References

Brown, C (2018) Aspiration. In Gilbert, I (ed) *The Working Class: Poverty, Education and Alternative Voices* (pp 38-63). Carmarthen: Independent Thinking Press.

Buck, A (2017) *Leadership Matters.* Woodbridge: John Catt Educational.

Morrish, A (2016) *The Art of Standing Out.* Woodbridge: John Catt Educational.

Nielsen, K, Randall, R, Yarker, J and Brenner, S-O (2008) The Effects of Transformational Leadership on Followers' Perceived Work Characteristics and Psychological Well-being: A Longitudinal Study. *Work and Stress*, 22(1): 16-32.

Rowland, M (2015) *An Updated Practical Guide to the Pupil Premium.* Woodbridge: John Catt Educational.

Scarlett, W, Chin Ponte, I and Singh, J P (2008) *Approaches to Behavior and Classroom Management: Integrating Discipline and Care.* London: Sage.

2. PASTORAL CARE

What is pastoral care?

Pastoral care is the backbone of a head of year's responsibility. All schools have a duty to safeguard and promote the welfare of pupils and one of your key roles as a head of year is to deal with this and to ensure they are educated in a safe and secure environment. You may, at times, feel as though you and your team are operating as social workers – although not true, there is a great deal of 'social' work involved in being a head of year. You will be the first point of contact for a number of staff, students, parents and external agencies, so a good understanding of the pastoral responsibilities of a head of year is vital if you are to succeed.

Much of your pastoral work will be aimed at solving problems and it is easy to become reactive to every issue without maintaining an overall strategic understanding of your pastoral role. As such, it is important that you develop key areas of your pastoral work and cultivate your year group's ability to manage issues on their own, giving you the freedom to tackle more serious issues that may arise.

Developing resilience

The school years can be incredibly challenging for your students and it is of vital importance that they develop resilience in order to deal with what lies ahead.

Building positive relationships is possibly the most important thing a head of year can do to improve resilience. Relationships where learners feel safe and valued help to strengthen resilience by allowing a student to feel supported while struggling with a given problem. The issue for a head of year is that you simply will not have the ability to build up strong relationships with your entire cohort immediately. This is where your tutor team will be invaluable. With your guidance they will understand why it is important for them to build relationships with their tutor groups.

Developing the autonomy of your students is another key skill for improving resilience. Heads of year can improve student autonomy by making sure that the focus is achieving manageable goals and targets for each student and not on drawing comparisons between other students. This ensures the worth of a student comes from them achieving what they set out to achieve rather than a competitive advantage over another student. Targets in subjects, for attendance or improving behaviour, can appear to stand in the way of autonomy for students. However, making sure they have clear and achievable goals will allow them to work towards what you are expecting. With this mindset embedded, students will feel the pride involved with reaching their goals, even if what they have achieved is less than another student.

While home environment is the biggest influencer on resilience (Center on the Developing Child, 2019), it is the one factor you as a head of year have little control over. However, goal setting and impulse control (being able to stop yourself from turning a thought into actions) have been demonstrated to have a significant impact on resilience (César Dias and Cadime, 2017). As a head of year looking to improve resilience, your work therefore needs to focus on goal setting through developing autonomy and tackling impulse control through behaviour support and therapeutic interventions.

Friendship issues

Friendship issues are one of the biggest factors in determining how a student will experience their schooling. As a head of year, you will be confronted on a regular basis with just how volatile teenage friendships can be and also the overwhelming impact they can have on all aspects of your role.

HOW FRIENDSHIP GROUPS FORM

Bruce Tuckman's forming, storming, norming and performing model (Smith, 2005) describes the stages a group will go through as it develops. Although for most this is a natural process, it is important that you as a head of year understand what is happening so that you are able to respond appropriately.

Forming

In this stage, most groups are positive and polite. Some are anxious and others excited; they do not yet understand their roles within the group. This stage can last for some time, as people start to work together, and as they try to get to know their new friends.

Storming

Next, the group moves into the storming phase, where people start to push against the boundaries established in the forming stage. This is the stage where many groups run into issues and will require a head of year to intervene. Storming often starts where there is a conflict between members of the friendship group. This can be because students have decided to challenge the authority of their appointed leader, or jockey for position as their individual roles become clear.

Norming

Gradually the friendship group will move into the norming stage. This is when people start to resolve their differences and appreciate their peers. This represents the group getting to know each other better and they begin at this stage to socialise more often together and are more identifiable as a friendship group.

Performing

When the group reaches the performing stage there is very little friction between members of the group and the group will be stable. It will feel easy to be part of the friendship group at this stage, and conflict will not be a regular part of the group dynamic.

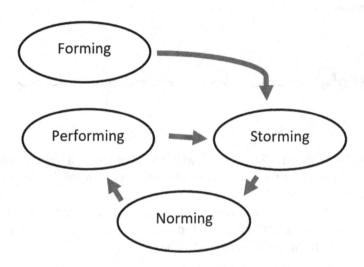

Figure 2.1 Tuckman's forming, storming, norming, performing model

Such is the nature of working with teenagers, the storming, norming and performing elements of the cycle will continue to occur regularly as new people join the group. Each new member might create a tussle for status, or others might see their role within the group of friends challenged. As a head of year, understanding how these friendship groups form and develop can help you to explore issues with the group in different ways and will also help you to acknowledge that friendship issues will always be a factor in the daily life of a secondary school.

PEER PRESSURE

Peer pressure is a powerful influence and can lead to students doing things that could appear to be out of character or represent a significant change in behaviour. Often this is led by a desire by students to not be ostracised from their friendship group. Education is key with peer pressure – ensuring that your year group is aware of what peer pressure is and that it is OK to say no when they don't want to do something can often be enough to stop an incident occurring. When peer pressure-related issues do arise, it is important that the student or students applying the pressure are tackled swiftly, in line with your school's behaviour policy, to ensure it doesn't continue.

CAUTION IS ADVISED

A lot of the issues that could be categorised as 'friendship issues' can be put down to normal teenage behaviour and every scenario you encounter will be slightly different due to the students involved. Therefore caution is advised whenever you have to get involved in a friendship issue. If you are too heavy-handed, the impact on those you are trying to help could be devastating for them, causing the initial issues to be exacerbated. Teenage relationships are intense in nature and any issues can weigh heavily on a student's mind. Likewise, not intervening in a friendship issue could lead to the development of a more serious bullying issue, which will be equally devastating for the students involved.

Case study

INTRODUCING NEW FRIENDS

Reena was a Year 7 student who was friends with Phoebe, who was the same age. Phoebe had been a constant presence in Reena's life since birth. Because of this, in their first term at secondary school, they would often refer to each other as best friends and go to each other's homes after school. The relationship seemed fractious at times, with Phoebe appearing to be more in charge in general. Problems arose when a new student, Liana, joined the year group and started to hang around with Reena and Phoebe.

Reena felt that Phoebe no longer wanted to be friends with her. As a result, she said to her parents that it made her feel very sad, that it made her not like herself, and that she wished she didn't exist.

Reena was worried that people in her year group had already developed close friendships and that she would be unable to make any new friends. Reena's head of year, Mrs Spencer, was worried by this scenario, as Reena and Phoebe had been friends for a long time and it was having a negative impact on Reena both in and out of school as she no longer socialised.

Mrs Spencer arranged to meet with Reena and Phoebe together and explored why they were no longer friends. She explained that every group of friends can struggle when a new person joins them and that giving up on a friendship when a new person has come along is not good for either of the students.

Mrs Spencer explained to the students that when a new person joins a group everybody has to adjust and must work together to understand how they will function as one group. The balance of the group had been upset by a new person joining (storming) but over time they would work out how to co-operate (norming) and eventually would have a strong friendship again involving all three students (performing).

Although this didn't solve the problem, it provided the students with an understanding of what is happening and what they needed to work on to move forward and stay friends.

The skill of listening

As a head of year, you will be expected to do a lot of talking. What is often forgotten about the role, especially its pastoral elements, is that you will also need to do a great deal of listening, to both staff and students. As a head of year you will become the problem-solver for a variety of stakeholders and it is important that you are able to listen effectively to the concerns of others. Done poorly, a listening exercise can leave parents feeling that you are inattentive to their needs and students feeling devalued.

A QUICK GUIDE TO LISTENING EFFECTIVELY

- *Concentrate on what the person is saying.*
- *Pay attention to words and body language; this can often tell you what someone is really feeling.*
- *Ask questions to clarify understanding.*
- *Respond with supportive noises not words.*
- *Have positive body language and make regular eye contact.*
- *Clarify the messages to ensure you have understood.*
- *Make it clear what the follow up will be.*

(Nathan, 2011)

You won't have answers to all the questions people ask of you. Instead you need to be able to signpost to other members of staff or external agencies as appropriate. Just by listening you have already shown that you value what the person is telling you and are building trust.

It is always advisable for you to be up to date on where to refer students, including any new services that may be opening in your local area. However, there is no shame in saying you will follow up at a later point once you have all of the information you need.

Conflict resolution

The problem-solving nature of your role as a head of year will inevitably lead into the realms of conflict resolution. That could be between students, staff and students or even the parents of students in your year group. It is important that you remain calm in any conflict resolution scenario and are equipped with the tools required to deal with such problems. It is also important to understand why people may attempt to resolve conflict on their own in five specific ways.

1. AVOIDING

Avoiding conflict is when a person perceives the discomfort of seeking a solution is greater than the discomfort of the conflict itself. This leads to people ignoring a problem or withdrawing from a conflict. As a head of year, it is important for you to realise that when conflict is avoided, nothing is resolved and avoidance is simply storing up issues for the future.

2. COMPETING

This is often associated with those who go into conflict with the aim of winning an argument. When someone is competing in a conflict, they expect everybody else to lose and don't allow room for other perspectives on a scenario or for compromise. As a head of year, you should always be on the lookout for those who have entered a conflict scenario competing to win. It is your job to alter this mindset and help them to accept other opinions on the matter.

3. ACCOMMODATING

Accommodating will look like one side of a conflict simply giving in and will at first glance appear to be a mature and well-reasoned response to a conflict scenario. As a head of year, you must act to ensure any accommodation is because of a newfound understanding of one another's perspectives on an issue. If this is not the case then it could lead to stored up issues for the future and a culture where the more dominant characters are able to dictate the course of future conflicts.

4. COLLABORATING

Collaboration is a healthier style of conflict resolution but is usually only apparent when each party is assertive in their views. Over time in these scenarios a group could learn to allow each person to share solutions to issues but as a head of year you must be careful that quieter participants are not being overshadowed.

5. COMPROMISING

When groups are compromising, each person has given up some of what they wanted to reach an overall solution. It is a fair way of reaching a solution but quite often not everybody is happy with the outcome and this could lead to future issues if someone feels they have been ignored or undervalued in the compromise.

POSITIONS. INTERESTS. NEEDS

Regardless of the style adopted by the parties involved in the conflict, as a head of year you need to know how to move the issue forward and allow for a solution to be reached. In order to do this, you will need to understand what the positions, interests and needs of those involved are. The positions, interests and needs – or PIN model – allows you to do just this, by structuring your conversations around these three key elements aiming to draw out common ground and progress to a solution.

Positions

The position of each student, teacher, parent or other stakeholder is basically what has led them to be in conflict. What are they disagreeing about? This is where you need to draw out what exactly each person involved wants to gain from this conflict.

Interests

The interests of each party involved in a conflict are what motivates them, such as having friends, being liked by your peer group or, in the case of a parent, wanting what is best for their child. It is important that when looking at interests you keep those involved focused on the conflict at hand and do not allow the conversation to stray into generic interests which have no bearing on the issue.

Needs

Needs represent the underlying drivers for each person involved in a conflict. These are often the basic human needs of safety, security and the right to be treated with dignity and respect. As a head of year, you need to help all parties in any conflict understand that many of their underlying needs are similar.

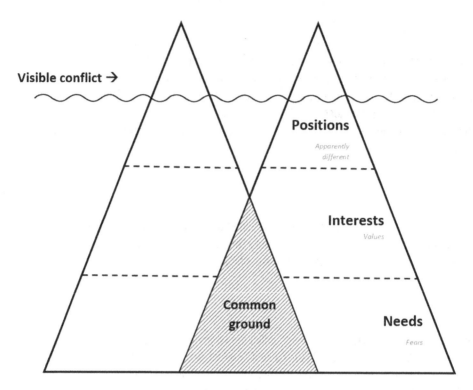

Visible conflict →

Positions
Apparently different

Interests
Values

Common ground

Needs
Fears

Figure 2.2 PIN model for conflict resolution

The aim with this model, originally developed by Andrew Acland (1990), is to begin the process of acknowledging those involved in a conflict have similar interests and needs. As discussion continues, each party will start to negotiate based on their interests rather than the initial position. This may lead to them identifying more areas of agreement in their interests and needs and reaching common ground over a given scenario.

Summary

As a head of year, you will deal with a number of pastoral issues for your students. The key skills of listening and being able to help them resolve conflict will be of vital importance in your role and will make sure you are giving students the best care. Having an understanding of how groups work together will allow you to diagnose friendship issues swiftly but also give you the knowledge to educate your year group in self-regulation of some of their lower-level issues.

Conflict resolution is a skill that needs to be practised and developed. However, spending time developing this not only will support you when dealing with students but is also an important skill to possess when dealing with challenging parents or disagreements between staff and students which will inevitably occur. As a head of year you will be called upon to deal with a variety of issues throughout the school and at the heart of everything you do must be the commitment to support the well-being of your year group.

Pastoral care is about more than just listening and resolving friendship issues, though these are at the core of many disputes. You also need to consider student well-being (Chapter 3), behaviour and engagement (Chapter 4), raising aspirations (Chapter 5) and bullying (Chapter 9).

❖ Reflections

1. How will you develop resilience in your year group and how will this support student well-being?

2. What are you going to do to support students in dealing with friendship issues? Can you identify a current issue that you could address? Think about how you might be able to help these particular students.

3. How can you teach your students to manage their conflicts?

4. Do you already demonstrate good listening skills? How do you know?

References

Acland, A F (1990) *A Sudden Outbreak of Common Sense: Managing Conflict Through Mediation.* London: Random House Business Books.

Center on the Developing Child (2019) *Resilience.* [online] Available at: https://developingchild. harvard.edu/science/key-concepts/resilience/ (accessed 9 March 2020).

César Dias, P and Cadime, I (2017) Protective Factors and Resilience in Adolescents: The Mediating Role. *Psicología Educativa*, 26(1): 37–43.

Nathan, M (2011) *A Pastoral Leader's Handbook: Strategies for Success in the Secondary School.* London: Continuum.

Smith, M K (2005) *Bruce W. Tuckman: Forming, Storming, Norming and Performing in Groups.* [online] Available at: http://infed.org/mobi/bruce-w-tuckman-forming-storming-norming-and-performing-in-groups/ (accessed 9 March 2020).

3. STUDENT WELL-BEING

What is well-being?

First and foremost it is important for you to understand exactly what well-being is. The Oxford English Dictionary defines well-being as *'the state of being comfortable, healthy or happy'.* This is a useful starting point, but you should recognise that well-being is more than 'in the moment' happiness. It is about feelings and how your students function within their environment. Most importantly it is about *'how they evaluate their lives as a whole'* (New Economics Foundation, 2012).

Poor well-being can have a profound impact on students throughout their school lives, from a one-off incident to more long-term and complex mental health concerns. It is clear that schools need to find ways to support students to achieve positive well-being.

The number of schools seeking help from mental health services has seen a sharp increase in recent years. In 2018 it was reported that the equivalent of 183 children every school day are referred to child and adolescent mental health services (CAMHS). As a head of year it is likely that you will be working alongside other professionals in your school, such as the special educational needs co-ordinator (SENCO) and support staff, in identifying students who are in need of additional support with their mental health.

There can be no doubt that school can be a difficult time for many – exam stress in particular can have a significant impact on the well-being of students – and it is for this reason that schools should encourage all pupils to work hard and achieve well, but make it clear that this should not come at the expense of their well-being.

Ultimately this chapter should make it clear that working on mental health is about more than just crisis intervention. The focus for you as a head of year should be on early intervention and embedding a culture of supporting student well-being.

Key issues in student well-being

SOCIAL MEDIA

There is a wide range of views on how much impact social media usage will have on a student's well-being. For some students, social media is viewed as a cause of anxiety, a platform for cyberbullying, and often as an addiction (O'Reilly et al, 2018). Others have found that platforms such as Twitter and Facebook allow students to escape from the external pressures that are threatening their mental health (Boyd, 2014).

Education is key in supporting student well-being around the use of social media. Ensuring that students understand the dangers of the internet is important, as is explaining that often what is seen is sometimes not a realistic worldview. Researchers have suggested that students who are relative novices at using social media are most likely to fall victim to the negative effects of social media usage but as their experience of the internet develops so does their ability to understand what they are viewing (Kraut et al, 2002). Teaching students how to use the internet is a key skill. It is true that many learners are probably more advanced with technology than some teachers, but the skill of being critical of what is seen online and interpreting things accordingly is something that you can help them to develop.

PHYSICAL AND MENTAL HEALTH

Health, both physical and mental, is an essential part of well-being and can enable or hinder students from achieving a proper sense of well-being. Unlike other elements of well-being, health is something that can only be tackled by other professionals who are suitably qualified. Early identification of issues through student–teacher relationships can help to provide an early indicator and allow a referral to be made.

This doesn't mean that as a head of year your role in physical and mental health is simply to make referrals. Issues such as healthy eating, exercise and education around the use of drugs and alcohol are things that can be delivered by you and your team within school. Although not directly resolving a health-related issue, such measures can raise awareness and help to reduce the likelihood of later health issues. They may improve a student's outlook and sense of wellness within themselves, which contribute to their overall well-being.

STABILITY OF HOME LIFE

An inescapable fact of working with children and young people is that their home lives will have a large influence on their well-being. External influences, which as a head of year you may have no control over, still contribute heavily to a student's well-being (Lupton, 2004). Where strong, positive familial relationships are present, a student will have a clear feeling of belonging within their family. This sense of belonging means that the student will feel their needs are being met, which contributes to a positive sense of well-being.

Family is important for providing love, advice and care. Unfortunately for a number of students this is not the case and family can also cause a strain on well-being through arguments, being critical and making too many demands. The impact of these stress factors can mean a student is more likely to become anxious and experience a poor sense of well-being (Pearlin, 1999). Stress can undermine mental health, meaning the pastoral support provided by you and your team will often serve as big protective factors in a learner's well-being.

As a head of year it is your job to foster an environment where students can build positive relationships with staff, which can help when there are issues with other adults in a student's life.

At times the stability of home life will fall into the realms of safeguarding. Chapter 8 looks at your role as a head of year when looking at safeguarding in more detail. However, you should speak to your safeguarding lead if the stability of a child's home life is a concern and you believe that it is impacting on their well-being.

Improving well-being

In order to develop a clear culture of promoting student well-being through your work as a head of year it is important that you have a clear understanding of what makes up 'good well-being' and how it can be implemented with your year group.

The model shown in Figure 3.1 for embedding a culture of well-being within your year group is an adapted version of the applied model for positive education (Norrish et al, 2013). It develops elements of earlier models of well-being in schools (Konu and Rimpelä, 2002) and shows how in order to experience well-being students must be able to experience and develop certain inner characteristics. The outer rings of 'Live it', 'Teach it' and 'Embed it' explain how you can develop a culture within your team and throughout your school to encourage student well-being.

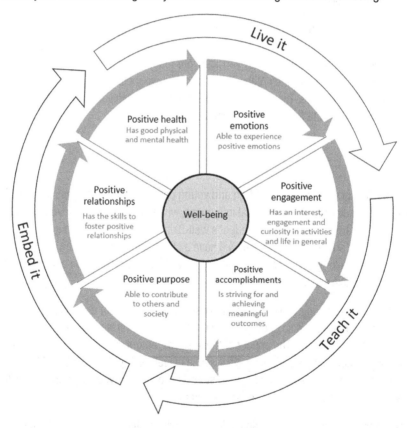

Figure 3.1 Model for developing student well-being in schools

LIVE IT

As a head of year you need to not only demonstrate to others what supporting student well-being is, you must also encourage other staff to buy into and 'live' the fundamental elements of well-being.

TEACH IT

You need to be teaching the well-being skills and characteristics in any teaching time you have control over, such as in PSHE or form-time activities, but also develop strategies that allow teachers to deliver the skills as part of the traditional curriculum.

EMBED IT

Embedding well-being involves its continued promotion across the school community, ensuring that clear processes are in place for staff to raise any concerns over well-being, and for any necessary actions to be taken by the appropriate person within the school such as a pastoral manager, SENCO or safeguarding lead.

WELL-BEING CHARACTERISTICS

The inner circle of well-being characteristics are what students need to experience in order to have a sense of well-being. Your job as a head of year is to ensure that your students have the opportunities to develop these characteristics. For example, publicly rewarding accomplishments for good work in a lesson allows students to experience both a sense of accomplishment and the positive emotion of joy.

Delivering a project-based group work session where students have the ability to build up new relationships and become curious and immersed in a short-term piece of work will allow the development of other key characteristics required to experience a sense of well-being.

The difficulty with the well-being characteristics is that many are linked to one another, so if one is not being experienced it is likely others will also be missing. Also, some characteristics such as physical health cannot be tackled by a head of year. Timely referrals to external agencies and contact with parents to raise concerns are just as important in ensuring good student well-being.

EMBEDDING STUDENT WELL-BEING

In a rural secondary school in Wales staff had recently been provided with an INSET session that focused on the need for all staff at the school, from the headteacher to the caretaker and the cook, to focus on the well-being of students and to look out for issues students might be facing that they may not be sharing.

The kitchen manager, Linda, had noticed that Xiao, a Year 8 girl, hadn't eaten for several days. Linda reported this to the head of Year 8 who then liaised with the school counsellor.

Xiao started seeing the school counsellor. Over the course of a few weeks they worked through Xiao's issues. It was discovered that she felt that she was overweight and needed to stop eating, which is why she had been avoiding her school dinners. The counsellor continued to discuss why this was the case with Xiao and it emerged that Xiao was a member of a group on social media that encourages teenagers to stop eating.

Despite knowing where Xiao had been accessing this material, the counsellor was making little progress and Xiao continued to not eat at school. It wasn't until she was able to have more intense support from CAMHS that Xiao began to improve and eventually started to eat at school again.

When she left school, Xiao recalled *'although my mental health continued to deteriorate, I felt comforted knowing my school was always there to help'.*

Summary

What the case study shows is that if the school had not begun their journey to embed the importance of well-being, this situation could have easily escalated and may only have been noticed by school staff at a much later stage. It also highlights the importance of sharing the responsibility for well-being between all staff at a school. As a head of year you may be instrumental in co-ordinating some of the work on well-being, particularly with your own year group, and could look to encourage a whole-school approach. Ultimately it must be everybody's responsibility.

The factors that can have an impact on a student's well-being are wide-ranging but in order for you as a head of year to improve your year group's well-being you need to be instrumental in developing a culture that promotes well-being and educates students on some of the key issues.

Social media, health and home life are given as key areas for concern. As a head of year you have a greater insight into your students' lives than many other teachers, therefore it is important that you are alert to potential issues and act to protect student well-being whenever you see an issue developing.

❖ Reflections

1. How can you embed well-being throughout your year group?

2. Exam pressure is often cited as one of the biggest issues affecting the mental health of students. What could you do to combat this?

3. How can you provide opportunities for students to be able to contribute to your school community?

4. Are students able to experience positive emotions while at your school? What do you do to ensure this is the case?

References

Boyd, D (2014) *It's Complicated: The Social Lives of Networked Teens.* New Haven, CT: Yale University Press.

Konu, A and Rimpelä, M (2002) Well-being in Schools: A Conceptual Model. *Health Promotion International*, 17: 79-87.

Kraut, R, Kiesler, S, Boneva, B, Cummings, J, Helgson, V and Crawford, A (2002) Internet Paradox Revisited. *Journal of Social Issues*, 58(1): 49-74.

Lupton, R (2004) *Schools in Disadvantaged Areas: Recognising Context and Raising Quality.* London: Centre for Analysis of Social Exclusion.

New Economics Foundation (2012) *Measuring Wellbeing: A Guide for Practitioners.* London: New Economics Foundation.

Norrish, J M, Paige, W, O'Connor, M and Robinson, J (2013) An Applied Framework for Positive Education. *International Journal of Wellbeing*, 3(2).

O'Reilly, M, Dogra, N and Whiteman, N (2018) Is Social Media Bad For Mental Health and Wellbeing? Exploring the Perspectives of Adolescents. *Clinical Child Psychology and Psychiatry*, 24(4): 601-13.

Pearlin, L (1999) Stress and Mental Health: A Conceptual Overview. In Horwitz, A V and Scheid, T (eds), *A Handbook for the Study of Mental Health: Social Contexts, Theories, and Systems* (pp 161-75). Cambridge: Cambridge University Press.

4. TACKLING BEHAVIOUR AND ENGAGING LEARNERS

The head of year's role in behaviour and engagement

As a head of year, it is likely you will spend a lot of time focusing on behaviour issues within your year group. Unlike in other middle leadership positions, you will need to understand how students are working across the school. What is often missing for a head of year's focus is how students are engaging with their learning not just how they are behaving. It is this shift in focus from noticeable secondary behaviour to the underlying engagement in learning that will help you to develop as a head of year and be better able to help your pupils.

Tackling behaviour

First, you must not underestimate the role you will play in tackling behaviour issues. As a head of year you are often one of the most visible authority figures to the students in your year group and other teachers will use you as an escalation point when they feel they are struggling to deal with a behaviour or when a student's behaviour has become an issue in more than one area of school life.

Much of your work in the area of behaviour will be around ensuring there is follow-up within your school's behaviour policy as well as supporting colleagues that need assistance with managing your year group within their classroom.

Being a head of year is a great responsibility. You are in a position where you can impact on the lives of every single student in your year group. Ultimately you are going to make a difference whether you like it or not; viewed in this way the standards and expectations you set for your year group are crucial. You set the tone for the entire cohort and the behavioural buck will often stop with you.

The follow-up to any incident is key. As a head of year, you should be wholly consistent in your approach to violations of the behaviour policy, sticking to the escalations of sanctions and ensuring any follow-up actions, such as restorative conversations, detentions and communication with parents and guardians, happen. Sticking to the processes shows students exactly what is expected of them and provides a consistent expectation of their behaviour around the school.

Behaviour as communication

Sixty per cent of all communication is non-verbal. For your students this means that their body language, gestures and even facial expressions in lessons and around the school are ways of communication. Imagine a student yawning during a geography lesson, or glancing at their watch as their form tutor tries to discuss an issue with them at the end of the day. This is all communication about how a student is feeling at a particular moment in time. Notably, students will often be unaware they have given non-verbal signals to their teachers and find themselves in trouble without fully understanding why.

Students actually rely heavily on non-verbal communication (Knapp et al, 2014). Sulking, eye rolling and play fighting can all be common behaviours during the school day. The students are trying to communicate with you and their peers through behaviour while they struggle to verbalise exactly what they need or how they are feeling.

More often than not this challenging behaviour manifests out of frustration at either not understanding a situation or not being able to verbally express their wants, needs and feelings. As students get older and consequently develop appropriate vocabulary, sentence structure and social skills, high level behaviour issues decrease. However, during the teenage years when hormone levels are changing, these behaviours can reappear without warning.

STUDENTS WITH SEND

Another thing that as a head of year you should have regard for is how students with special educational needs and disabilities (SEND) communicate with their peers. Often language difficulties and the anxiety surrounding interaction are at the root of a student's behaviour and these issues can be heightened for a student with SEND.

As many as 40 per cent of students displaying behavioural issues may have undiagnosed communication problems. In Wetherby Young Offenders Institution, research found that around 60 per cent of inmates had speech, language and communication needs (Bryan et al, 2015). As a head of year, you need to judge for yourself whether you believe it is a coincidence that these young people who have developed extreme behavioural problems also suffered from communication difficulties.

Seventy-five per cent of young people who have social, emotional and mental health (SEMH) problems also have communication problems (Henecker, 2005). It is with this in mind that you must approach behaviour problems within your year group. Think logically about why the behaviour has occurred, what the students are trying to communicate and if there is an underlying reason for the behaviour.

Don't be afraid to ask for support from SEND colleagues; you will often be able to spot a pattern in behaviour long before others would within the school, and it could stop a student's educational journey being derailed. Looking at behaviour through this lens ensures you are focused on supporting the students in your year group and not simply trying to punish them at every slip up.

Keep your cool

With the pressure of your role it can be easy for you to feel like you have lost control. The most important thing to remember is to not 'blow your top'. Avoid losing your temper at all costs. Try not to raise your voice too much and don't give emotional responses to behavioural issues (Bennett, 2010). This, of course, is an act; you are a human being so will experience a range of emotions when dealing with issues. When you react in an emotional way, you demonstrate a lack of control and this can affect how you are perceived by students. They may believe they have got under your skin or got the better of you. Long-term, this can cause damage to the authority a head of year holds. At all times a head of year should follow up properly and promptly in line with the school's behaviour policy without making a scene. Dealing with behaviour issues away from the crowd and without shouting does little to impress upon a wider group of students but deals skilfully with the needs and behaviours of the individual student. This consistent approach means your students know exactly where you stand on behavioural issues and that you will always follow up. Ultimately, you are the gatekeeper to the behaviour system for your year group.

Engaging students

Engaging students in their learning is the whole reason you work to tackle behaviour. There are three types of engagement: emotional, cognitive and behavioural (Appleton et al, 2008), all of which need to be understood by you as a head of year if you are to engage your students in their learning and begin to bring about changes in behaviour within your year group.

- **Emotional engagement** is how the student feels about their learning but also about their life in more general terms. For example, feeling emotionally safe in school or buying into what is happening in school and therefore feeling connected to their learning.
- **Cognitive engagement** is what the student is thinking about in the classroom and depends on the strategies implemented by teachers or the activities the students are involved in. For example, the student is thinking about what he or she is being taught rather than something outside of school.
- **Behavioural engagement** refers to the actions of the student, which is the most noticeable form of engagement of the three. For example, the student completes the work they have been given and appears to be focused.

THE ENGAGEMENT HIERARCHY

Before any other type of engagement can occur, students must first emotionally engage in their schooling. As a head of year, you play a pivotal role in getting this fundamental step in engagement right. You are the link between the issues from a student's personal life and their learning in the classroom. When this first step of helping students to emotionally engage is missed, students are more likely to be looking for an easy answer to problems that they face, and this can lead to students giving up or refusing to take part in the first place. They do not want the challenge of learning something new.

Only once emotional engagement is secured can cognitive and behavioural engagement be tackled and improved. When students are emotionally engaged in something they are more likely to think about it. This is cognitive engagement. Cognitive engagement is important because students only remember what they think about (Almarode and Miller, 2018). If a student is thinking about something, such as the content of a lesson, they are more likely to take action and complete a task based on that information. This is behavioural engagement, the most noticeable form of engagement. Where there is a lack of this form of engagement, poor behaviour is what the classroom teacher will notice first. As a head of year, you must remain aware of the fact that a lack of behavioural engagement is often an indicator of deeper issues.

FIVE STEPS TO IMPROVING ENGAGEMENT

There are five steps (see below and Figure 4.1) that a head of year can take in order to help improve engagement, all of which aim to tackle the emotional engagement of students. This allows for improvements in cognitive engagement and finally in behavioural engagement. In order to sustain engagement, a head of year must constantly assess how students are working, how they are feeling about their work and more importantly be ready to respond to any unfolding and newfound needs of the students. Ultimately, engagement is fostered through a robust ethos which is headed up by you as the head of year and demonstrated daily throughout your work.

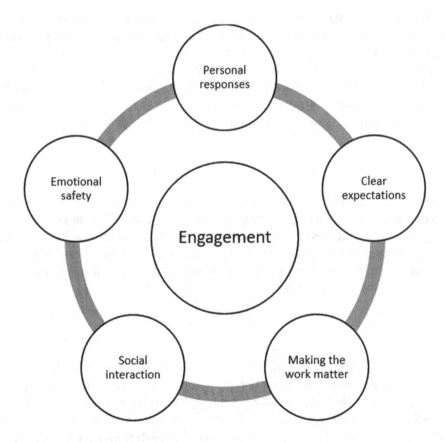

Figure 4.1 Five steps to improving engagement

1. Personal responses

Allowing students the chance to use their own personal experiences and expertise in the learning environment through the conversations they have is one way you can begin to incorporate personal responses into education. In the classroom you could provide students with the option to create their own analogies or metaphors, allowing them to select how they will share their responses to a question (eg, writing, drawing, speaking, etc), or allowing students to select the context in which a concept is explored (eg, selection of a habitat, constellation, simple machine, or variables for an independent experiment). These examples have one thing in common; they allow students to personalise their responses to meet their background, interests or expertise (Reschly et al, 2008). Although much of this is focused on what could be done in the classroom, as a head of year you are able to provide many learning activities that go beyond the classroom but also have the ability to influence the practice of others within your school.

2. Clear expectations

As a head of year, you will have been told countless times that you must have high expectations of your students. However, this doesn't necessarily mean being a stricter version of yourself. Instead the word *high* needs to be substituted for *clear*. When you have inexplicably high standards, you create a situation where students are always hoping to hit whatever target you have in mind but often find themselves falling short. With clear expectations, students know what success looks like and have success modelled to them throughout their learning. Not only does this show students clearly what is expected but allows them to achieve the standard they have been set.

3. Making the work matter

You need to create opportunities for students to see that their work can matter to someone other than their class teacher and their academic reports. This can be achieved through a number of teaching and learning strategies including co-operative and group working. However, as a head of year, it is unlikely you will be involved in the day-to-day teaching for your whole year group. Instead you can look to introduce opportunities for community-based projects that allow your students to have an impact on the classroom, school or wider local community.

4. Social interaction

How often do you think about the opportunities that are provided within your school for social interactions? It seems simple: break times, lunchtimes and during discussion in lessons all provide opportunities for social interaction. The value of nurturing these social interactions cannot be overstated. As a head of year, you should seek to provide students with opportunities to talk about their learning and interact with their peers. This supports their ability to ascertain meaning from their work and aids development of conceptual understanding.

5. Emotional safety

Emotional safety is the element of engagement that should be viewed as most important. Put simply, it tackles the question 'does the student feel safe?' However, it is about more than physical safety. As a head of year you need to foster an environment where students feel comfortable to ask questions and make mistakes. If students feel threatened in the learning environment, if getting things wrong is too high-stakes, then students will simply disengage. Preservation of self takes precedence over everything else in these scenarios and is a sure-fire way to stop students from engaging in their education (Skinner et al, 2009).

Case study

At a large inner-city school, problems had developed with students truanting lessons or being removed from class for disrupting lessons. Heads of year were asked to join in a corridor patrol during lesson-time. Staff at the school reported feeling more supported in their lessons.

The heads of year felt that they had to lead by example because many of their interactions with students were now in the view of other teachers. The heads of year worked on modelling conversations with students and kept their conversations focused on engagement with learning and not the immediate behavioural issue being presented.

Over time the number of referrals decreased, and heads of year reported that they were able to spot patterns of behaviour where students were being removed from lessons and not engaging a lot quicker.

In particular there was a situation where a teacher who was giving detentions to students who didn't answer test questions correctly was facing a number of behavioural challenges from the class. The head of year who was walking the school checking on behaviour at the time spoke to the teacher's head of department about the issue and explained to them that the high-stakes questioning was leading to a number of students refusing to engage in order to protect themselves. The head of department explained this to the teacher who agreed to change to a low-stakes method of questioning where students completed exit tickets. The teacher was able to see who did and didn't understand the work and the students felt able to engage in the lesson.

Summary

As a head of year, you will be the first port of call for teachers who are struggling to manage the behaviour of the students in your year group. It can be very easy to become focused on punishing poor behaviour, moving students quickly through a series of ever-escalating sanctions. Your school's behaviour policy will dictate what path these sanctions follow, which is often set above the level of head of year. Your main focus therefore should be on identifying exactly why problem behaviour is occurring, including what the underlying motivational factors that are stopping students from being engaged with their learning are. Most importantly, you should be looking for solutions to issues surrounding engagement and encouraging other teachers to do the same.

Viewing behaviour through the lens of engagement allows you as the head of year to respond more appropriately to the needs of your students and also means that you deal with underlying problems which could become more deep-seated and difficult to work with.

Much of the work a head of year will do around promoting engagement and tackling behaviour will be to set the standard, model it and foster an environment that promotes engagement from your year group. There will always be times when students choose to not engage in their education, and at times there will be no underlying cause that you can discern. Students are unpredictable in their nature. It is your job to provide the consistency they need to make sense of the learning environment.

❖ Reflections

1. **Are you clear about your role and expectations within your behaviour policy?**

2. **How have you made your standards clear to your year group?**

3. **Is there a process in place for you to discuss concerns around behaviour with the SEND team? If not, how could you approach this?**

4. **How can you as a head of year create opportunities for structured social interaction to aid engagement?**

References

Almarode, J T and Miller, A (2018) *From Snorkelers to Scuba Divers: Making the Elementary Science Classroom a Place of Engagement and Deep Learning.* Thousand Oaks, CA: Corwin Press.

Appleton, J, Christenson, S and Furlong, M (2008) Student Engagement with School: Critical Conceptual and Methodological Issues of the Construct. *Psychology in the Schools*, 45(5): 369–86.

Bennett, T (2010) *The Behaviour Guru: Behaviour Management Solutions for Teachers.* London: Continuum.

Bryan, K, Garvani, G, Gregory, J and Kilner, K (2015) Language Difficulties and Criminal Justice: The Need for Earlier Identification. *International Journal of Language and Communication Disorders*, 50(6): 763–75.

Henecker, S (2005) Speech and Language Therapy Support for Pupils with Behavioural, Emotional and Social Difficulties (BESD) – a Pilot Project. *British Journal of Special Education*, 32(2): 86–91.

Knapp, M L, Hall, J A and Horgan, T G (2014) *Nonverbal Communication in Human Interaction.* Boston, MA: Wadsworth.

Reschly, A, Huebner, E and Antaramian, S (2008) Engagement as Flourishing: The Contribution of Positive Emotions and Coping to Adolescents' Engagement at School and With Learning. *Psychology in the Schools*, 45(5): 419–31.

Skinner, E, Kinderman, T and Furrer, C (2009) A Motivational Perspective On Engagement and Disaffection: Conceptualization and Assessment of Children's Behavioral and Emotional Participation in Academic Activities in the Classroom. *Educational and Psychological Measurement*, 69(3): 493–525.

5. RAISING ASPIRATIONS

Varied aspirations

As a head of year, you will be well placed to improve the aspirations of your year group. This area of your work is complex, as many of your students will already have varying levels of aspiration and be influenced by any number of internal and external factors in their lives.

With this in mind, some 'norms' appear to have developed within education such as white British pupils often having lower aspirations than other ethnic groups and being the least likely to remain in full-time education (Stahl, 2012). Or that underachievement is more prevalent in boys than girls (Ison and Weatherburn, 2007), leading to many teachers and observers of educational discourse labelling students as having 'low aspirations'.

Your role is to break down these stereotypes, which are deeply entrenched in society, to give students whose experiences of life are limited the new experiences they need, and to allow all students to have aspirations that are not limited by their social standing or other attributes that are out of their control.

One often overlooked element is the focus on the day-to-day aspiration to improve one's own current situation. Having the aspiration to try and improve a piece of classwork, falling attendance or negative behaviour is arguably more important than longer-term aspirations as it is more likely to lead to an overall positive movement towards a student's future career or educational goals.

THE WHITE WORKING CLASS

White working-class students have continued to be some of the lowest attaining groups across the country for some time, although the link between aspirations and being white and working class is not clear (Sutton Trust, 2016). Government ministers have highlighted a deeply embedded culture of low aspiration as a significant cause of anti-social behaviour and academic underachievement (Gillborn, 2009).

As a head of year, you are responsible for finding a way to shift the culture of low aspirations and help your students set high aspirations for themselves. This is no mean feat when research suggests that students are influenced heavily by their understanding of social class (Skeggs, 2002). Much of what forms a student's aspirations comes from a student's self-perception of what others from a similar background can and will achieve in later life. This suggests that one of the key roles of a head of year in raising aspirations is to break the connection between the perceived limitations of your student's upbringing and their aspirations.

You will need to expose your students to success stories from a wide range of socio-economic backgrounds and develop the idea that everybody is able to achieve. Likewise, it is important that students from white working-class areas, or indeed any other areas where there is deprivation, are trained to aim for continuous self-improvement in order for them to break through the glass ceiling holding them back.

BOYS VERSUS GIRLS

Research has suggested that gender-specific ideas about certain jobs often have an overbearing impact on future aspirations (Chambers et al, 2018). Boys overwhelmingly aspire to take on roles in traditionally male-dominated sectors and professions and girls aspire to traditionally more female-dominated professions.

This can particularly manifest itself when it comes to subject choices when picking GCSEs to study and is even more evident when it comes to making applications for further education, higher education or apprenticeships after school. At points your role as a head of year will be predefined: schools now often have a clear drive on encouraging girls to engage with STEM (science, technology, engineering and mathematics) subjects. However, students could feel that they are being pushed down a certain path when these 'whole school' interventions take place. Although at surface level it would appear the aspirations of your cohort are set high, in reality they may become disinterested and lose the focus on continuous self-improvement. Rather than having high aspirations, they are paying lip service to the school and feeling their own aspirations slip away.

It is therefore very important that as a head of year, you bridge the gap between these two extremes. Although employed by the school to carry out its set policies, you hold a unique position where you also support your cohort of students in a pastoral sense and can spend time understanding what drives them and ultimately what their aspirations are.

Resilience and its role in raising aspirations

Resilience is the key to raising aspirations, both long-term and in the present day. Unfortunately, many schools view resilience as nothing more than an inspirational quote on a wall, such as one that is often attributed to Winston Churchill: *'Success is not final, failure is not fatal: it is the courage to continue that counts.'* What is perhaps missed from these good-natured decorations is a deeper understanding for the students at your school about what it means to make a mistake, learn from it and continue to improve.

As a head of year, you need to make developing resilience a key component of your plan for improving your year group. For this to really happen, students need to experience making mistakes, but also be able to swiftly make improvements in a *'high challenge – low threat'* (Myatt, 2016) environment where they are driven to improve consistently while the comeback for not getting something right is minimal. It needs to be OK to make mistakes and learn from them.

The same is also true of behaviour and attendance issues. Students will make mistakes and misbehave in school or even pretend to be ill to have a day off. What you need to do is ensure your students are equipped to improve on their current situation, for which resilience is key. It is all too easy to become stuck in the role of a 'naughty' student or a low attender; it is much more difficult for students to identify that they need to improve on their behaviour and then actually do it. The support of a strong head of year when doing this will be invaluable.

New experiences

In order to fully appreciate the vast options open to them, your students need to gain life experience that shows exactly what is on offer once they leave school. Sadly, a number of your students may have had very few experiences outside of their local area. This in itself can limit what options your students believe are available to them.

There will always be students who attend every trip abroad and those who do not. You may be able to find some funds to support students in accessing these experiences but ultimately you will struggle to stop the inequity. Instead, you should work strategically to identify students who have not been involved in school trips before and look to involve them in other activities that give them an exposure to something new while remaining in school.

I am not suggesting that heads of year should be devoting chunks of time to delivering excursions to other countries or to events outside of the local town. Trips and excursions are incredibly valuable in helping to give your students new experiences but it is also possible to bring new experiences into your school. Chances to explore future careers through interactive workshops at school can be just as useful as visiting an industry employer's site – for example, a company who provides a hands-on operating theatre workshop can give your students a positive experience of working in a clinical setting without leaving the school.

Likewise, the experience of being involved in the planning of a school building project could be just what a student needs to raise their aspirations and to start seeing a reason for improving their work in school.

Not just aiming for university

Schools can often be biased towards driving students towards a university education. As a head of year who undoubtedly received a university education, you are likely to contain within yourself this same bias. Your own experiences of education will always have an impact on how you advise your students.

What is important for students is for them to understand all of the options that are available to them when they leave school, particularly when viewed as a tool for achieving their aspirations. For some an apprenticeship or technical qualification would be much more valuable than a loosely related

A level qualification. By having access to the full range of possibilities, your students are more likely to have raised aspirations to improve their day-to-day work at school because they have a clear idea of what they need to do to achieve their goals.

You need to be vigilant for students being pushed into paths that are not compatible with their aspirations as this could cause students to disengage from their learning and lose focus on day-to-day improvements. It is OK to suggest alternatives to students and allow them the opportunities to explore them fully but ultimately students need to be working towards their own aspirations.

Case study

Harrison was a 14 year-old student who had always wanted to be a physiotherapist. Mrs Amin, Harrison's head of year, noticed that his attendance had dropped along with his grades in numerous subjects. She spoke to Harrison about her concerns and he admitted that he had been having time off and that in his lessons he was struggling to keep up. He also said that he didn't see the point in some of his GCSE subjects.

Mrs Amin booked Harrison an appointment with the school's careers adviser who explained that in order to gain a place on a physiotherapy course, Harrison would need to gain at least a grade 5 in his GCSE subjects. The careers adviser also set Harrison up on a one-week placement at a local sports club where he was able to see exactly what a physiotherapist did.

The result was Harrison understanding what he needed to do in order to reach his goal of becoming a physiotherapist. This led to an improvement in his day-to-day aspirations, and to Harrison asking his teachers how he should improve his work when he made mistakes.

Summary

The relationship between aspirations and attainment is not very clear in research. In general, approaches to raising aspirations have not translated into increased learning (Education Endowment Foundation, 2018). However, as a head of year you are responsible for more than just the learning outcomes of your year group. You are also responsible for how they develop as people.

Young people usually have high aspirations for themselves. What they need from you and your team is the knowledge and skills to progress towards their aspirations.

The attitudes, beliefs, and behaviours that surround aspirations in disadvantaged communities are diverse. Researchers have highlighted some factors that could be at play, but ultimately it is difficult to generalise about students and their motivations. Instead, your aim should be to ensure your work does not limit the aspirations of your students and that you allow them to work at improving the knowledge and skills they require in making progress.

The biggest focus for raising aspirations should be around developing the aspiration to continuously improve one's self. It is through the aspiration to do better that more long-term aspirations start to develop. Without wanting to do better, other aspirations become unobtainable and students lose engagement.

❖ Reflections

1. What new opportunities can you expose your year group to?

2. How do you ensure students are able to maintain a variety of aspirations, not just going to university?

3. How can you ensure your school equips student with the knowledge and skills required to make progress towards their aspirations?

4. Consider how you can monitor the impact on attainment of any interventions or approaches.

References

Chambers, N, Kashefpakdel, E T, Rehill, J and Percy, C (2018) *Drawing the Future.* London: Education and Employers.

Education Endowment Foundation (2018) Aspiration Interventions. In *Teaching & Learning Toolkit*. London: Education Endowment Foundation.

Gillborn, D (2009) Education: The Numbers Game and the Construction of White Racial Victimhood. In Pall Sveinsson, K (ed) *Who Cares About the White Working Class?* (pp 15–22). London: Runnymede Perspectives.

Ison, L and Weatherburn, M (2007) *Gender and Education: The Evidence On Pupils in England.* London: Department for Education and Skills.

Myatt, M (2016) *High Challenge, Low Threat: Finding the Balance.* Melton: John Catt Educational.

Skeggs, B (2002) *Formations of Class and Gender.* Nottingham: Sage.

Stahl, G (2012) Aspiration and a Good Life Among White Working-class Boys in London. *Journal of Ethnographic & Qualitative Research*, 7: 8–19.

Sutton Trust (2016) White Working-class Boys Have Lowest GCSE Grades as Disadvantaged Bangladeshi, African and Chinese Pupils Show Dramatically Improved Results. Press release, 10 November 2016. [online] Available at: www.suttontrust.com/news-opinion/all-news-opinion/white-working-class-boys-have-lowest-gcse-grades-as-disadvantaged-bangladeshi-african-and-chinese-pupils-show-dramatically-improved-results/ (accessed 20 April 2020).

6. DRIVING ATTENDANCE

Why do some students have poor attendance?

Poor attendance in a school context is anything that falls below 95 per cent, as this is the number used by the government when looking at the impact attendance can have on progress (Taylor, 2012). There can be a whole host of reasons for a student's attendance to fall below this level, from medical issues through to bereavement or even a family holiday (see Table 6.1).

However, there will be students who have poor attendance who do not present with one of these clear-cut reasons for being absent from school. As a head of year, along with your colleagues, you will need to investigate the reason for any attendance issues and create a plan to tackle them.

The Department for Education (previously called the Department for Education and Skills) conducted research looking at this very issue and set out some of the perceived reasons parents and carers gave for poor attendance alongside reasons schools suggested.

Table 6.1 Reasons for absence from school (Malcolm et al, 2003)

PARENTS/CARERS	SCHOOLS
· BULLYING	· PARENTS NOT VALUING EDUCATION
· PROBLEMS WITH TEACHERS	· DISORGANISED LIFESTYLES
· PEER PRESSURE	· INADEQUATE PARENTING
	· LOW STUDENT SELF-ESTEEM

What is clear is that where attendance is concerned, the family and school appear to be at odds and in some ways blaming one another. However, what needs to be found is the underlying reasons for absence.

Figure 6.1 below outlines some of these possible underlying reasons.

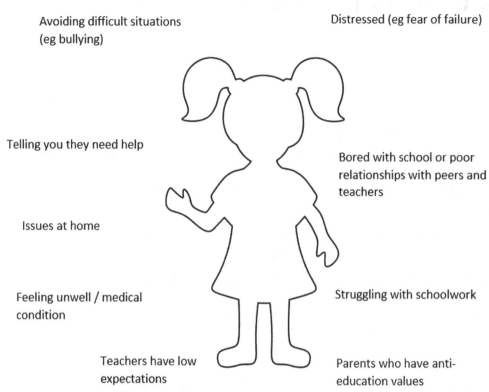

Peer pressure

Avoiding difficult situations
(eg bullying)

Distressed (eg fear of failure)

Telling you they need help

Bored with school or poor
relationships with peers and
teachers

Issues at home

Feeling unwell / medical
condition

Struggling with schoolwork

Teachers have low
expectations

Parents who have anti-
education values

Figure 6.1 Student-focused reasons for absence from school

What is very important when looking at the reasons for poor attendance is to ensure that issues are dealt with quickly. Research has shown that where a swift response doesn't occur, issues often snowball and become greater (Reid, 2014, 2008). A friendship issue can quickly escalate into bullying, worrying about reprisal and parents feeling more galvanised in their desire to protect their child by keeping them at home.

The implications of poor attendance

The most obvious implication of poor attendance is the impact it will have on progress (Mortimore et al, 1988). Quite simply, if a student isn't present in the classroom, they will not be learning the same as those who are present. Without the required knowledge, the ability to make progress will be diminished and over time the impact of this will be more severe.

There are, however, social implications of being absent from school too (Galloway, 1985). A student who misses out on time at school is also missing out on time with their peers who are in school for most of the day. Over time this could lead to issues within friendship groups, a student withdrawing from a group and becoming isolated or even a student becoming anxious about returning to school at all.

What is of further concern to you as a head of year is why the student is able to have so much time off in the first place. Are they at home with the support of parent? Are they caring for parents or other relatives? Is the home environment so disorganised that the family are simply unaware of how much education has been missed? Naturally some issues surrounding attendance will fall into the remit of your safeguarding lead. Attendance is often a good indicator for how things are in a student's home life.

Improving attendance

PREVENTION

As with most things, prevention is better than cure, meaning that it is easier to stop something happening in the first place than to repair the damage after it has happened. Therefore, the preventative work you do as a head of year to maintain attendance is crucial.

Day-to-day initiatives

First and foremost, once you have a clear plan about what attendance initiatives you will be running (such as rewards, student reports, parental meetings) you need to make it public. Raise the profile of attendance so everybody in your year group is on board, or at the very least aware that attendance is being taken seriously.

You may wish to consider using key members of staff or visitors to explore the importance of good attendance with your students in an assembly or group-work session, maybe even delivering lessons on good attendance where students need to identify causes and consequences of poor attendance. What is important is that you start to raise the aspirations of your students around their attendance (see Chapter 5).

Communicate with home about attendance but do more than just explain your school's target for attendance; provide parents with information on sleep, health or use of social media. Make it clear how different factors can have an impact upon attendance and provide advice on how to create better routines to support the students in your year group.

Part of your day-to-day work with attendance will be to ensure students are able to build positive relationships with staff members, particularly their tutors, and also to recognise where a student has good attendance or has improved their attendance. Doing so publicly will also aid with raising the profile of attendance.

Data analysis

Although each school will have its own data systems in place, there are some key pieces of information that as a head of year you will need to understand.

First, you will need to be able to analyse each student's overall attendance and be able to account for any 'approved educational activities' such as educational visits and sporting events. It is important that you include the approved activities as part of the student's overall attendance. You will need to be able to identify the percentage attendance of each student but also of the year group as a whole and any subgroups within it. For example, look at each tutor group within a year, vulnerable groups (such as pupil premium, looked after children and SEND students) and finally individual students.

When analysing your data, one group of students should stand out and be of concern: those who are persistently absent and have an attendance rate of 90 per cent or lower (Department for Education, 2019). This is a government-set limit and students in this category are at risk of seriously underachieving and suffering other implications of missing days at school.

EARLY INTERVENTION

As with most things, it is best to intervene early when you spot that a student's attendance is starting to drop. Often simply noticing this and having a conversation with the student and their family is enough to identify any issues and get attendance back on track.

What you should aim to do at this point is create an action plan with the student and their family about how you can address barriers to the student attending school. These could be issues such as hunger, access to health care, homelessness, transportation or other challenges. You must look to increase their engagement with school by working to tackle some of these barriers.

TARGETED INTERVENTION

Inevitably for some, the early interventions will have no impact and attendance will continue to drop. At this point the interventions you will offer as a head of year will become more targeted at specific issues or concerns that have been raised by the student, their families or school staff.

Engaging external agencies

Where it becomes clear that the school's interventions are not having the desired impact it may become necessary to request the support of other agencies or groups of professionals. Often each local authority area will have its own support mechanisms in place.

In most areas this includes a professional who is able to work with the family outside of school, identify the barriers to education and complete more involved work to help the student and their family resolve the issues. These professionals can take a variety of titles depending on the area of the country in which you live, but each local authority will have an attendance team able to provide you with information on the support services available to your students.

LEGAL INTERVENTION

Unfortunately, where no improvements are forthcoming local authorities will pursue legal options in tackling the attendance issue. This most often takes the form of an education penalty notice (EPN), which is a fine for not securing a student's regular attendance at school, but it can escalate up to a custodial sentence.

Education penalty notices

EPNs can be issued for a number of reasons but principally when a pupil has failed to attend school for at least five days (or ten sessions). An EPN will also be issued should the student go on holiday during term time and it is possible to receive a holiday EPN and an irregular attendance EPN within the same time period (Department for Education, 2019). Although as a head of year you will have no control over penalty notices, it is important that you are able to explain what the process of events is likely to be to any parents during your discussions surrounding attendance.

Case study

Dante was a Year 8 student whose attendance was at 94 per cent. Dante's head of year highlighted him as someone who needed to be targeted for intervention to stop his attendance dropping further.

Dante was placed into a mentoring programme where he met once a fortnight with a member of staff that he trusted, his form tutor Mr Boyle. At their meetings, Dante and Mr Boyle discussed what was causing him to miss days of school. Dante explained that he struggled getting out of bed in the mornings and that once he was running late then he didn't want to come to school and get a detention.

Mr Boyle discussed this with Dante's head of year and a meeting was arranged to discuss a plan. During the meeting it was felt that the family could do with some extra support with establishing a night-time routine for Dante and his younger siblings. Dante's head of year agreed to give him a reward if he attended school every day for the next two weeks. A support worker spent time after school working with the family to build routines such as putting away games consoles an hour before bed and setting an alarm to give Dante enough time to get ready.

Dante successfully attended school every day for two weeks and received his reward. His head of year agreed a new reward for the end of term should Dante's attendance continue to improve.

Summary

Attendance is a complex area of work for a head of year because it is the area where you will feel least able to have an impact because it brings together many different elements that make up a student's life.

The causes of poor attendance are wide-ranging, yet at their heart sits a student not able or willing to attend school due to a yet-to-be-discovered barrier to learning. Your job is to create an environment where students can express their concerns and have issues dealt with before they escalate into bigger issues causing students to have time off school.

It is vital that you don't think you have to know the solution to every student's issues; your job is to identify there are issues and where necessary work with other professionals to seek a resolution. Each attendance case is different, and no solutions will be the same, yet being able to get a child back into school will have a positive impact on the student's life.

❖ Reflections

1. How will you raise the profile of attendance within your year group?

2. How will you recognise good or improved attendance? Is it sustainable over the course of a school year?

3. Are systems in place to monitor attendance data and are you able to act upon the information you receive?

4. How can you work with other professionals to support your students and their families?

References

Department for Education (2019) *School Attendance and Absence*. [online] Available at: www.gov.uk/school-attendance-absence (accessed 9 March 2020).

Galloway, D (1985) *Schools and Persistent Absentees*. Oxford: Pergamon Press.

Malcolm, H, Wilson, V, Davidson, J and Kirk, S (2003) *Absence from School: A Study of its Causes and Effects in Seven LEAs*. London: Department for Education and Skills.

Mortimore, P, Sammons, P, Stoll, L and Ecob, R (1988) *School Matters*. Berkeley, CA: University of California Press.

Reid, K (2008) The Causes of Non-attendance: An Empirical Study. *Educational Review*, 60(4): 345–57.

Reid, K (2014) *Managing School Attendance: Successful Intervention Strategies for Reducing Truancy*. Oxon: Routledge.

Taylor, C (2012) *Improving Attendance at School*. London: Department for Education.

7. CELEBRATING ACHIEVEMENT

Celebrating achievement

Celebrations of achievement have become very common in schools up and down the country and the basis for this is often found in a school's behaviour policy. Rewards are designed to improve behaviour and encourage students to work harder.

Often rewards will be based on some form of points system where students can win a prize if they collect a certain number of points, essentially teaching students that if they do X they will get Y (O'Brien, 2018).

Rewards have a similar effect on behaviour as grades do on feedback, where pupils may ignore comments when marks are also given (Butler, 1998). This means students will often find the easiest way to gain rewards without intending to create any real change within themselves or their behaviour. In the worst cases students will only do something good if they will be rewarded.

The power of recognition

Your students are motivated by acknowledgement, praise and positive reinforcement; more so than material rewards, which offer some positive feelings that fade quickly (Dix, 2010). Your work in celebrating success has much to do with creating a culture of recognition of good work whereas attempts to 'reward' students can undermine their intrinsic motivations (Baranek, 1996).

Simple acts of recognising students' efforts or an exceptional piece of work will make them feel good. This makes it more likely they will perform the same positive actions again. Grand gestures create an environment where one student receives all the rewards while others who may have put in the same amount of effort do not. Where the odds are in favour of a student not being recognised justly for their work, the amount of effort put in may decrease.

Consistency in recognising positive work or behaviours within your school should be a priority. Where students know they will be recognised for doing the right thing, they are more likely to do it (Harkness, 2011). Other students notice that they are not being recognised and up their game, thus leading to an overall improvement in behaviour and engagement while also creating a more positive ethos.

Ways to celebrate success

VERBAL PRAISE

Verbal encouragement and praise are the easiest ways to motivate and celebrate a student's success both in lessons and in general around the school. Verbal praise can be used for a variety of behaviours. It can be used before a tough piece of work to encourage participation or immediately afterwards to celebrate the student completing a piece of work they have struggled with. Naturally, something that is beyond what was expected should be praised, be that completing additional work, creating an exceptional piece of work, trying hard when struggling or even holding doors open.

NOTES, POSTCARDS AND CERTIFICATES

Notes, postcards and certificates work in a similar way to verbal praise but should be used where a piece of work is truly above and beyond what was expected. The physical nature of one of these forms of praise means it will stick with the students for longer and means the student can share their success with others.

CONTACT WITH PARENTS/GUARDIANS

Parents and guardians love it when a teacher acknowledges their child's accomplishments. When teachers share positive acknowledgements with parents/guardians, typically the comments are excitedly discussed with the student at home. Just like with other forms of praise, this allows the student to share their successes with those that mean the most to them and helps to reinforce positive behaviours and attitudes. Contact with parents can be achieved in multiple ways, most schools provide a text messaging service, letters or postcards sent home with the student or in the post. However, the most effecting way of communicating with home is by phoning parents directly; research suggests that this is by far the most appreciated method of communication for parents and your students (Payne, 2015). Don't leave praise just for parents' evenings; taking the time to make note of positive behaviour and hard work makes it all the more special.

YEAR GROUP CELEBRATIONS

Wanting to do well for their peers can be a great student motivator, so having a reward system that allows you to recognise the successes of the students in your year group with the rest of your cohort is important. It not only helps to recognise and celebrate students but creates a bond between peers, contributing to a better overall ethos within your year group. Just as with other forms of celebration, giving physical rewards and prizes alongside acknowledgement and certificates can lead to students losing the focus on the intrinsic nature of being recognised and wanting to be successful.

PEER RECOGNITION

Recognition from a student's peers can be very powerful and you should seek out opportunities to have your year group give praise to one another. One way this can be achieved in small groups is using a 'strength circle'. To begin, each student will need their own envelope with a blank piece of paper inside. Each student should write their name on the outside of their envelope and then pass their envelope to the student on their right. With each passing of the envelope, students should take the piece of paper out of the envelope and write down a strength they recognise in their peer. Encourage students to write about a specific time they noticed each person's strengths or positive contributions to their time at school.

DISPLAYING WORK

Displaying students' work in classrooms or around the school on celebration boards is an excellent way to celebrate their achievements. Students feel a great sense of self-worth when something they have written or created is posted up for others to see in a prominent place in the school.

AWARDS CEREMONIES

Hold an award ceremony to recognise student achievement at the end of the year. Awards should be thoughtfully considered and based on each student's personal growth, character and achievements. These should be presented as awards in their own right with a certificate, with parents, school staff, school governors or community figures invited to demonstrate the importance of each student's contribution to the school. Avoid presenting the awards alongside a physical prize, as this can remove the intrinsic nature of receiving recognition.

SOCIAL SHARING

Almost all schools have a website and even social media profiles. In such a digital age you have an opportunity to share the achievements of your students publicly. Celebrate the achievements of your students through sharing pictures of their work, a short celebration video highlighting the contributions to the school from a group of students and possibly even include a message from you as a head of year or the headteacher to show how important their work is to the school. Not only does this work to increase the self-worth of the students being praised, it acts as a target for others to aspire to within your year group and allows the wider community to see the good work taking place at your school.

Consistency is king

This chapter has already touched on the importance of being consistent in recognising and celebrating success. Where students know they will be recognised for doing the right thing, they are more likely to do the right thing and work harder. This is noticed by other students who also want to be recognised and so their effort, quality of work and behaviour also begin to increase.

What can undo all of your hard work in celebrating achievement and recognising your students is a lack of consistency. Nothing will damage the trust between you and a student more than when a student has done everything asked of them and where there would normally be an acknowledgement, there is nothing. You must ensure when you begin to add in ways to celebrate achievement that they will be manageable and sustainable. The best plans, policies and strategies can all be undone if your students don't believe that the system will be followed.

Case study

Zeke was a Year 7 student in a small coastal town high school. He had a reputation for misbehaving and he reported that his teachers often expected him to misbehave so didn't give him a chance.

At the end of a difficult parents' evening, Zeke and his father spoke to Mrs Thorne, Zeke's head of year. She explained that while many of the things said by the teachers were correct, Zeke was also a very talented student who was often found helping the younger students at lunchtimes, getting them involved in activities and sorting out their problems. After this, Zeke agreed he needed to turn his behaviour in lessons around.

The following day Zeke arrived at school early, and as he made his way to his form room he held a door open for a teacher. He didn't get a response so mockingly shouted 'you're welcome'. Zeke was immediately issued with a detention for being rude.

After finding out that Zeke was already in a detention, Mrs Thorne went to find out what had happened. After hearing the story she reminded Zeke's teachers that every day should be a fresh start and that when he does things right, it needs to be acknowledged. Mrs Thorne explained how recognising small improvements will enable Zeke to continue doing the right thing and over time they will see an improvement in his behaviour. She also stressed that almost all students will have slip-ups and these shouldn't be used as opportunities to stop acknowledging positives.

Over time Zeke gained a reputation for being very courteous to staff on the corridors by holding doors open and saying good morning. Although only a small gesture, it was recognised by his teachers which led Ms Eyre, Zeke's science teacher, to call home and compliment him on being such a good role model to others.

The act of recognising a small positive behaviour allowed for a great improvement over time for Zeke. However, if this recognition had been inconsistent then the work could have easily been undone.

Summary

Time and again research finds that the simple phone call home has one of the greatest effects on promoting positive behaviour and engagement from students (Payne, 2015). It supports the notion that students are motivated by acknowledgement, praise and positive reinforcement rather than by material rewards (Dix, 2010) and that they like to share their successes with their families and peers.

You need to create a clear plan of which recognition tools you will use with your year group. Once you have decided these they must be followed through relentlessly. Consistently doing what you agreed to will over time build a positive climate for learning within your year group and lead to students being motivated to improve their work and do the right thing simply because it makes them feel good.

As a head of year you hold a position where you can not only apply your own rewards and acknowledgements but influence the practice of others within your school. Where possible you should aim to include all staff working with your year group in your celebration plans and allow them to contribute positive experiences from their own areas of the school.

❖ Reflections

1. **Does your current rewards system provide materialistic rewards or more intrinsic and longer-lasting acknowledgement of success?**
2. **Which recognition tools do you plan on using with your year group and how often will these take place?**
3. **What is in place to recognise day-to-day achievements?**
4. **How can you make sure your new celebrations for achievement are maintained?**
5. **Are there any barriers to keeping this consistent you need to be aware of? (For example, ordering postcards, assembly hall being used for exams.)**

References

Baranek, L (1996) *The Effect of Rewards and Motivation on Student Achievement.* Allendale, MI: Grand Valley State University.

Butler, R (1998) Enhancing and Undermining Intrinsic Motivation: The Effects of Task-involving and Ego-involving Evaluation on Interest and Performance. *British Journal of Educational Psychology*, 58: 1–14.

Dix, P (2010) *The Essential Guide to Taking Care of Behaviour.* Harlow: Pearson Education.

Harkness, S K (2011) *Consequences of Rewards: The Creation, Perpetuation, and Erosion of Social Inequality.* Stanford, CA: Stanford University Press.

O'Brien, J (2018) *Better Behaviour: A Guide for Teachers.* London: Sage.

Payne, R (2015) Using Rewards and Sanctions in the Classroom: Pupils' Perceptions of Their Own Responses to Current Behaviour Management Strategies. *Educational Review*, 67(4): 483–504.

8. SAFEGUARDING

Safeguarding is everyone's responsibility

Safeguarding and promoting the welfare of children is everyone's responsibility (Department for Education, 2019) and as a head of year, you fulfil a vital function in ensuring the students in your year group are kept safe.

Successful safeguarding is wholly reliant upon individual professionals at all levels assuming responsibility and taking action in line with your school's safeguarding procedures whenever they suspect there is a safeguarding issue (Pengelly, 2013).

Your school's designated safeguarding lead (DSL) will be the first point of contact for all safeguarding concerns. However, as a head of year you need to pay close attention to the information to which you have access and understand exactly how you may be able to spot emerging patterns, which can highlight issues in the lives of your students.

What should you look out for?

As a head of year, you are in a unique position of being able to observe the broader picture of how students are engaging with their time at school. You are also one of the first points of contact for issues outside of school. This bigger picture, beyond what every member of staff at your school will be taught in safeguarding training, allows you to look out for anything that may cause concern so you can spot developing issues and alert the DSL.

CHANGES IN BEHAVIOUR

There are a number of behavioural changes you may notice as a head of year; after all, one of your roles is to monitor the behaviour of your year group. Not all negative or positive behaviours are the result of a safeguarding concern. What a head of year may spot, however, are unexplained changes in behaviour or personality, with a student potentially even becoming uncharacteristically aggressive (NSPCC, 2019). These could become clear through your own analysis, but some behaviours may be less obvious to you and will be noticed by your tutor team, such as a pupil becoming withdrawn or seeming anxious. You may become aware of these through requests to add students to interventions which are under your control.

ATTENDANCE CONCERNS

Attendance can be another indicator of underlying issues. The reasons for a drop in attendance can be wide-ranging, from a student lacking social skills or having few friends to running away or going missing (NSPCC, 2019). It should also be noted that attendance can sometimes signal that a student is a young carer and is spending time at home to care for parents or siblings (Nathan, 2011). It can also be an indication of medical needs which will require additional support in order for a student to attend school.

PROGRESS IN SUBJECTS

A decline in progress within a number of subjects can be an indication of students becoming less engaged in their education. This can, of course, be a natural development within a student's life or a response to an acute issue around friendships or a personality issue with teachers. Should the issue be apparent across a number of subjects, dramatic in its nature (eg, going from high flyer to scoring few or no marks in an assessment) or sustained over a long period, then further investigation may be needed.

COMMUNICATION WITH PARENTS OR CARERS

As a head of year, you will be one of the key relationships between home and the school. This allows you to build a good understanding of a student's relationship with their parents. The relationship between parents and student can be an indicator of safeguarding issues (NSPCC, 2019). Therefore, it is important that you listen carefully to what parents are saying to you during their discussions with you. It is not uncommon for parents to be open about times when they are struggling with their children and this can often be a request for help. If you feel that this is the case then you might consider referring the family to support services that can work closely with them to tackle issues. It is always suggested that you discuss concerns with the DSL before making a referral as this may form part of a bigger safeguarding picture.

INFORMATION FROM OTHER AGENCIES

Perhaps most obviously, you may be provided with information from external agencies who you have engaged to work with students. Due to external staff not being teachers, some students will be more comfortable in sharing information with them. Should an external agency give you information that causes concern, it should be reported to the DSL and advice sought about any action you need to take. It is important that you thank the member of staff who gave you the information and let them know who the DSL is should they have any further concerns.

If you have been involved in setting up the counselling for a student, you are not entitled to know what is discussed with a counsellor. Although you may ask a student how the counselling sessions are going, you must never ask what is discussed as this could break the trust between student and counsellor.

Multi-agency working

Depending on your school procedures, and under direction from senior staff including the safeguarding lead, a head of year may be expected to attend a meeting with other agencies and represent the school. Your role means you have a good understanding of the students in your year group and your knowledge of the support available within your school means you are able to suggest support options that might be available.

A CHECKLIST FOR ATTENDING A MULTI-AGENCY MEETING

- Check that the information you have about the student is accurate.
- Go with an up-to-date picture of the student's attendance, any behavioural concerns and progress information.
- Speak to the student's form tutor. Although you may not be able to share the reasons for a meeting taking place, they will be able to give you any information from their observations and conversations with the student each day.
- If you have lessons or duties that will need to be covered before attending a meeting, make sure you have everything in place for your absence.
- Make clear notes on what has been discussed; official minutes from meetings can take some time to reach you and you need to make sure actions you agree are completed.
- Report any decisions that are made in the meeting to the DSL.
- Remember you are representing your school so be professional; be sure to raise any of your concerns in a factual manner.
- Be honest about what you and the school are able to offer the student and their family. Do not over-promise.

Looking after yourself

It is important for you to realise that through your role you may be made aware of the struggles in a student's life and be a party to some upsetting information. This can take its toll on you personally, meaning it is important for you to get support when you need it.

Dealing with difficult situations can leave you feeling isolated as a head of year; there are few staff members you can talk to about safeguarding issues, which could mean your usual support structures may not be able to help. It can also be easy to feel like you have a lack of clarity over how you should be working (Turnbull, 2005). In these situations it is important that you identify who you can speak to about issues and seek some supervision from someone able to support you.

Non-managerial supervision (meaning it is not intended to be an administrative or managerial task) is the process used to debrief and discuss the difficult scenarios you may be dealing with in your role and will enable you to look at how you can develop your practice, as well as ensuring you and your students are being supported (Thompson and Gilbert, 2011). Unlike in supervision with your line manager, this 'non-managerial' supervision focuses on the safeguarding and pastoral tasks you have been asked to complete, situations you have encountered and how you feel these situations are being managed. It provides you with an opportunity to share how you are dealing with issues and to alert someone who can help if you need support yourself.

If this person is not the DSL, it is important that you check first what you can and cannot share with them to ensure you are working within the school's safeguarding policy. Where the person you work with as a non-managerial supervisor is someone who should not be aware of specific safeguarding issues, you must ensure you do not discuss specific cases and that you maintain the confidentiality of the students' families and the staff with whom you work.

Case study

Abigail's father had COPD – a progressive lung disease – which had been getting worse over the course of the year. The family informed the school at the start of the year that Abigail was occasionally late to school because she was giving her father his medication.

Following a family breakdown, Abigail's mother moved out of the family home and her father became dependent on Abigail. This led to an increased number of absences from school, all of which were covered by a note but which became increasingly frequent and had an impact on Abigail's educational progress.

When Abigail's head of year contacted the family to discuss the situation they felt that Abigail's father was clearly preoccupied with his deteriorating health. Without Abigail's mother at home, the head of year was concerned that Abigail's attendance would continue to decline and wanted to put support in place for Abigail.

After discussing the case with the DSL, an education welfare officer was asked to visit the family at home, check the situation and look for ways to offer support. Meanwhile, the head of year identified ways to support Abigail in school, including engaging the support of a local young carers group.

Summary

As a head of year, you are in a position to spot changes in a student's life that may go unnoticed by others. Your job, therefore, is to remain vigilant to any changes in your students and be aware of the pastoral support options you are able to offer. Ultimately, you must have regard for your school safeguarding policies and raise all of your concerns with the DSL.

Should you attend any multi-agency meetings, be sure to prepare yourself properly and go armed with the facts surrounding how the student is performing at school and the support options at your disposal.

It is most important to ensure you support yourself. Dealing with difficult situations can take a personal toll on you as a head of year. Therefore, seeking support from suitable colleagues is necessary to ensure you can complete your job well.

It is possible that all of the possible indications you may encounter as a head of year are merely a reflection of the turbulent personalities of your teenage students. However, it is always best to discuss any concerns with your school's DSL as they may have additional information, meaning your concern is part of a much wider picture.

❖ Reflections

1. How does your role fit within your school's safeguarding policy?
2. Do you have ways of spotting changes in students' behaviour, attendance and progress?
3. Are you aware of the support options available to your students?
4. How can you go about supporting your own well-being?
5. Who in your organisation would be a suitable 'supervisor' to support you in dealing with difficult situations?

References

Department for Education (2019) *Keeping Children Safe in Education: Statutory Guidance forw Schools and Colleges*. London: Department for Education.

Nathan, M (2011) *A Pastoral Leader's Handbook: Strategies for Success in the Secondary School*. London: Continuum.

NSPCC (2019) *Spotting the Signs of Child Abuse*. [online] Available at: www.nspcc.org.uk/what-is-child-abuse/spotting-signs-child-abuse/ (accessed 9 March 2020).

Pengelly, R (2013) *What Every Manager Should Know About Safeguarding Children*. Surbiton: Grosvenor House Publishing.

Thompson, N and Gilbert, P (2011) *Supervision Skills: A Learning and Development Manual*. Lyme Regis: Russel House Publishing.

Turnbull, A (2005) Using Line Management. In Wise, C and Harrison, R (eds) *Working with Young People*. London: Sage.

9. BULLYING AND CYBERBULLYING

Defining bullying

Bullying is a high-profile area of your responsibility as a head of year. You must be acting to prevent bullying and be tackling it immediately where it occurs. Bullying is the repetitive, intentional hurting (physically, verbally, emotionally, psychologically) of one person or group by another person or group, where the relationship involves an imbalance of power (Anti-Bullying Alliance, 2019). It includes name-calling, hitting, pushing, spreading rumours, threatening or undermining someone and can happen anywhere, not just in school (NSPCC, 2019). It can be carried out in person or remotely; for example, through social media. Although primarily you will be dealing with in-school issues, you may also be drawn into out-of-school issues that have found their way into school.

Bullying can take different forms or be called different things. Some common examples are as follows.

BAITING

Baiting is intentionally making a person angry by saying or doing things to annoy them. It can be used to antagonise those who might be bullying others to get them to join in the bullying, or used by a bully to try and get a person to react negatively so that they get into trouble.

BANTER

The dictionary suggests that banter is *'the playful and friendly exchange of teasing remarks'*. However, it can be used by students to intentionally be hurtful towards another student, occur repetitively over a period of time or involve a power imbalance, which means banter can easily become bullying.

FALSE FRIENDSHIPS

False friendships can be difficult for adults to spot. With a false friendship one student will pretend to be friends with another but uses their power to bully the other student. This is particularly difficult because the victim will not want their 'friend' to get into trouble. The Anti-Bullying Alliance suggest that some children are more likely than others to fall victim to a false friendship, such as students who are disabled (Anti-Bullying Alliance, 2019).

What is the legal framework for dealing with bullying?

Schools do have some powers set out in law when dealing with bullying. Section 89 of the Education and Inspections Act 2006 provides that maintained schools must have measures to encourage good behaviour and prevent all forms of bullying among pupils.

Within the Equality Act 2010 is the Public Sector Equality Duty, which came into force on 5 April 2011 and covers age, disability, gender reassignment, pregnancy and maternity, race, religion or belief, sex and sexual orientation. This means schools need to eliminate unlawful discrimination, harassment, victimisation and any other conduct prohibited by the Act, as well as foster good relations between people who share a protected characteristic and people who do not share it.

In addition, schools need to have their own policies in place to prevent bullying and to deal with bullying where it occurs. As a head of year, you will be one of the key people within a school tasked with educating students about discrimination and acceptance of differences, and when bullying happens you will be at the forefront of investigating issues and ensuring everybody feels supported in the process.

Tackling bullying

Working in a school, you will already hold the view that preventing and tackling bullying is vital and should be the responsibility of every member of staff who encounters bullying. Ultimately, one of the most important elements of tacking bullying includes a highly visible school ethos and clear policies that staff are trained to implement (Cooper Gibson Research, 2018).

Your school will set out in its behaviour policy how bullying should be sanctioned and after an investigation, often completed by you as a head of year, these sanctions should be put in place. What is important in these cases is that sanctions are consistent but also that some work goes into addressing the underlying issues between the students.

Although bullying within school can be upsetting for those involved, once it is out in the open there are often witnesses and it is easier to detect. Where bullying is taking place via the internet or through mobile phones it can take much longer to detect and investigations can become more complicated.

What is cyberbullying?

Cyberbullying is bullying that takes place online. Although initially this may appear to be a lesser form of bullying because there is no physical element, online bullying can follow the child wherever they go, via social networks, gaming and mobile phones. This means it has the potential to affect your students throughout their days and can lead to severe emotional distress.

Due to the nature of cyberbullying, it is likely to transcend the natural confines of the school day. Regardless of when bullying is occurring, you must act to support your students and remember that during the school day the students involved are brought together, intensifying any pre-existing issues.

Restorative approaches

Restorative approaches aim to improve and repair relationships between students and should form a key part of your anti-bullying strategy. However, before looking at how you should make use of restorative approaches, you must remember that bullying involved a power imbalance between one or more of your students and this power imbalance must be managed by whomever is leading a restorative meeting or conversation.

Restorative approaches generally have four key elements: respect, responsibility, repair and reintegration (Hendry et al, 2010).

- Respect for everyone by each person listening to other opinions and learning to value them.
- Responsibility – each person taking responsibility for their own actions.
- Repair – developing the skills within the school community so that its individual members have the necessary skills to identify solutions that repair harm and ensure behaviours are not repeated.
- Reintegration – working through a structured, supportive process that aims to solve the problem and allows young people to remain in their lessons.

Key questions to structure restorative conversations (Education Scotland, 2017) might be as follows:

- What happened?
- What were your thoughts at the time?
- What have been your thoughts since?
- Who has been affected by what happened?
- How have they been affected?
- What do you need to happen now?

Through a restorative conversation the focus is shifted from the bullying behaviour to the impact the behaviour has had on the students involved. This shift can be difficult for the victim but it is important to work through these difficulties to educate the student doing the bullying to recognise the impact of their behaviour and to bring about change.

Working with parents

There are two polar opposite approaches that can be taken when looking at the role of parents when dealing with bullying.

In previous years, some schools have used the 'no blame' approach, where discussing a bullying incident with parents would be discouraged (Minton and O'Morre, 2004). Advocates for this approach believe that students need to take responsibility for their own behaviour and where necessary modify it. However, you will already be aware that parental involvement in behaviour issues is a powerful tool that can have positive outcomes in terms of bringing about behavioural change.

It is important for you to note that all parents of students involved in bullying or being bullied will experience a mixture of emotions towards the situation. The parents of the victim will often be concerned about making sure their own child is OK, but also have a strong sense of justice needing to be served. Likewise, a parent receiving a call or being brought into school to be told their child has been involved in bullying another student could become angry, upset or even confused at the situation.

No parent intends for their child to become a bully and it is difficult to view their own child in this way; therefore, you will also need to support these parents in understanding the scenario but also how they can move forward from the issue and support their child in modifying their behaviour.

Peer mentoring

School-based peer mentoring is an intervention that can have a positive impact on a range of issues affecting student well-being. Your school may already have an established peer-mentoring group or it may need to be created by you. Either way the benefits of peer mentoring are difficult for a head of year to ignore.

There is consistent evidence that young people who have experienced peer mentoring demonstrate higher levels of satisfaction with life in general, increased self-esteem and improved peer relationships and become happier at school as a result (Mentoring and Befriending Foundation, 2010).

As a head of year, you will need to first ensure any students working as peer mentors have been suitably trained in areas such as reporting concerns, listening sensitively to others and how to offer appropriate advice. Once the foundations of good training have been completed there are a number of models for peer mentoring that have been used in schools around the country.

For some schools a drop-in style system works well. Peer mentors have a set location where they will be during social times and students who need their support are able to seek them out. This scenario has been known to work best where younger students are experiencing issues and can lead to potential bullying issues being noticed and reported to staff much sooner.

Another model for peer mentoring sessions is to have dedicated time within the week where targeted students are given an appointment to meet with their mentor to discuss how their week at school has been. This can take place during tutor time, social times or even during lessons and can help you to ensure students you are worried about are able to speak to a mentor without having to initiate the contact.

Ultimately, you will need to decide what will work best in your school. Having an established peer mentoring group means that there are more opportunities for bullying issues to be identified and for early recognition of issues that could later lead to bullying, such as a friendship issue or being new to a school. This isn't designed to replace the need for the more thorough approach that will need to be taken by teachers where bullying is happening but provides additional support to victims and detects issues that would have otherwise been missed until they escalated.

Building an anti-bullying culture

Arguably, the most important thing you can do to help tackle bullying in your school is to build a strong anti-bullying culture within your year group. To do this you will need to focus on developing three key areas of your year group: values and norms; relationships; and expectations (see Figure 9.1).

VALUES AND NORMS

The values that you espouse will undoubtedly match with core British values of democracy, the rule of law, individual liberty and mutual respect. The link with British values provides a clear framework on which to base a school or year group value system. The most important thing in the context of anti-bullying is mutual respect and tolerance of those with different faiths and beliefs. The rule of law links with what has previously been discussed on the legal context of bullying within schools and how some bullying can be aimed at protected characteristics.

Celebrating the differences between members of your year group and demonstrating how different cultures, faiths and beliefs help build up our identity as a nation will go some way to establishing that everybody is respected and valued within your year group.

Making it the norm to accept differences, to challenge views that seek to oppress others and to allow your students to be a proactive force in supporting one another when they are facing difficulties is again crucial for 'setting out your stall' in the anti-bullying context.

RELATIONSHIPS

There are two elements surrounding relationships and an anti-bullying culture. First, you will need to have developed positive relationships with members of your year group and have mutual respect embedded throughout your interactions with students. Second, you and your team should be educating your students on what makes a healthy peer relationship and how to handle disagreements. Through educating students on what a positive peer relationship is and modelling it through your own actions, you embed that positive relationships are at the heart of daily life in your year group.

Cultural expectations will be based on your school's behaviour and anti-bullying policies, but how you express what those expectations are to your year group is important. As a head of year you will be responsible for ensuring the behaviour expectations for your year group are clear. When focusing on bullying, you should ensure the expectations on your students are equally clear. What do you expect them to do when they think someone is being bullied?

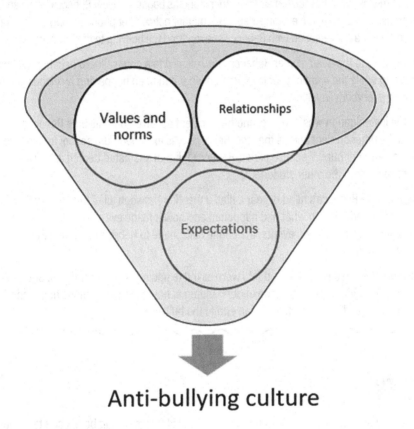

Figure 9.1 Building an anti-bullying culture

Taken together, these three key areas of values and norms, relationships and expectations create a clear anti-bullying culture in which students are able to feel safe and supported by teachers and their peers. It also helps to dissuade those who might display bullying behaviour, as it is clearly not an acceptable way of doing things within this culture.

Rebecca's first few years of high school were difficult. She had moved to a new school and while the majority of students were welcoming, some members of her tutor group would write nasty notes about how she looked and how she had been 'clinging on' to other friendship groups.

Over time this behaviour escalated and the other students began to follow Rebecca home and make prank calls late into the evening. Rebecca's mother noticed her phone ringing and Rebecca ignoring it. After a conversation with Rebecca she reported the bullying to the head of year.

After speaking to the head of year Rebecca was referred to a counsellor to help her deal with the bullying while the head of year investigated what had been happening by discussing the issue with everybody involved.

While the investigation was ongoing, another incident occurred but this time Rebecca slapped the other student across the face. Rebecca was excluded from school for a day for assaulting another pupil. Because of this, Rebecca felt that she hated herself and wished she could have ignored the other students.

After some time Rebecca's head of year called a meeting between all of the students involved where they talked through what had happened and how it made everybody involved feel. The conversation focused on two events: the phone calls made to Rebecca and then Rebecca slapping another student.

At the end of the meeting, both students were asked to apologise to one another. Both students did apologise but it was the understanding of how their own actions had made the other student feel that helped to bring an end to the bullying.

Summary

Often bullying goes unchallenged for a prolonged period of time so it can be difficult to identify individual incidents where a victim has been made to feel that they are being bullied.

As a head of year, you need to make sure any investigations into a bullying incident are thorough and include as much detail as you can find out about previous incidences of bullying. Simply sanctioning the student who has been bullying another will not resolve the situation. Although it may serve as a deterrent, often the bully has not realised the emotional harm they have caused, as this is less evident than physical harm. By using a restorative approach, you are helping to make sure that the bully is educated in how their actions have made other people feel as well as helping the victim to feel they are being listened to and are empowered in the process.

Creating a culture within your year group where it is not acceptable for anybody to be bullied is of paramount importance. When the anti-bullying culture is right, many issues will be brought to the surface much quicker and dealt with before they become more sustained. Likewise, where you have support structures in place such as peer mentors, you will be able to detect any concerns much sooner and act upon this information.

Every head of year will experience a bullying incident at some point; what sets apart the good heads of year is the swiftness of the response and the overriding culture of their year group.

❖ Reflections

1. Do you understand how your work dealing with bullying links with the law?

2. Are you knowledgeable on the use of restorative approaches for dealing with bullying? Outline the specific restorative approach within your school.

3. What support mechanisms are in place to support your students with bullying issues?

4. How do you teach your students what makes a healthy friendship?

5. What are your year group's core values and how do they help prevent bullying?

References

Anti-Bullying Alliance (2019) *Tools & Information.* [online] Available at: www.anti-bullyingalliance.org.uk/tools-information/all-about-bullying/what-bullying (accessed 9 March 2020).

Cooper Gibson Research (2018) *Approaches to Preventing and Tackling Bullying.* London: Department for Education.

Education Scotland (2017) *Restorative Approaches.* [online] Available at: https://education.gov.scot/parentzone/additional-support/specific-support-needs/social-and-emotional-factors/Restorative%20approaches (accessed 9 March 2020).

Hendry, R, Hopkins, B and Steele, B (2010) *Restorative Approaches in Schools in the UK.* Cambridge: Economic and Social Research Council.

Mentoring and Befriending Foundation (2010) *National Peer Mentoring Anti-bullying Pilot 2008-10.* Manchester: Mentoring and Befriending Foundation.

Minton, S J and O'Morre, M (2004) *Dealing with Bullying in Schools: A Training Manual for Teachers, Parents and Other Professionals.* London: Paul Chapman Publishing.

NSPCC (2019) *Bullying and Cyberbullying.* [online] Available at: www.nspcc.org.uk/what-is-child-abuse/types-of-abuse/bullying-and-cyberbullying/#bullying (accessed 9 March 2020).

10. DEALING WITH MAJOR EVENTS

Warning

The case study in this chapter features a local school's response to pupils affected by the Manchester Arena bombing. It contains some detailed descriptions, so please be aware of this if you have been affected by any issues related to terrorism or terror attacks.

A student's response to trauma

A major event is one that is frightening and potentially dangerous for your students either to be involved in or to witness. For your students, their sense of safety depends on the perceived safety of their attachment figures and themselves. Anything that threatens this perceived safety could be classified as a traumatic experience.

Traumatic experiences can bring about strong emotions and physical reactions that can persist long after the event. Your students may feel terror, helplessness, or fear, as well as physiological reactions such as heart pounding, vomiting or loss of bowel or bladder control. Students who experienced an inability to protect themselves or who lacked protection from others to avoid the consequences of a traumatic experience may also feel overwhelmed by the intensity of physical and emotional responses (van der Kolk, 2014).

Despite the best efforts of parents, carers and school staff, traumatic situations still occur. This trauma can come from outside of the student's family, such as natural disasters, car accidents or community violence. Likewise, they can come from within the family, such as domestic violence, physical or emotional abuse, or the unexpected death of a loved one.

Although this chapter attempts to look at a number of traumatic incidents, there are many issues that will not be covered. What you as a head of year should be focusing on is how, in general terms, you can respond to a traumatic event and support your students. Many of the actions needed will be generic and applicable in a number of scenarios and only you are best placed to judge what is needed in an individual case.

family breakdown

An increasingly common scenario you will face as a head of year is the separation of parents. Although on the face of it this may not look like a traumatic incident, for your students this can have a devastating impact on their normal life, routines and sense of belonging.

Possibly the most difficult part of supporting a student going through a family breakdown is for them to begin facing the finality of separation (Hall, 2011). In coming to this realisation, students will be dealing with a number of feelings that are not dissimilar to those associated with bereavement. Although it isn't advised for you or any member of staff to sit a student down and bring them to the realisation that their family unit is irreparably broken down, consideration should be given to allow the students the opportunity to speak to professional counsellors about their feelings. For some a referral to a counsellor may be a step too far and simply having a trusted adult to talk to will suffice.

Because of the very personal nature of a family breakdown, previous work on developing positive relationships between staff and students is vital to ensure you are able to fulfil the role of a trusted adult who can listen to issues.

There are, of course, more practical matters to bear in mind when dealing with a family breakdown. For example, new living arrangements and routines for the student and what impact this may have on their journey to and from school and who you should contact in an emergency. Although this is a difficult time for all of the family, it is important that you establish the facts around these key issues as soon as possible so you can allow the family time to come to terms with the breakdown and also support the student while they are in school.

Similarly, in a practical context, contact from school should be made to both parents. Both parents have a right to be involved in their child's education unless a court order stipulates otherwise. As a school you must ensure both parents are contacted and consulted on any number of issues. For example, sending reports home, arranging parental meetings, first day calls for absences and who should be informed about behavioural issues.

Bereavement

The death of a loved one can be devastating and affects people in different ways. For your students it is important that they understand that there's no right or wrong way to feel. They could be in school and presenting in the same way they would have done at any other time. Alternatively they could experience and display a whole range of very powerful emotions. It is also possible for students to experience emotions unexpectedly and to switch between appearing fine and then experiencing strong emotional outbursts.

Experts generally accept there are four stages of bereavement:

1. *accepting that the loss is real;*
2. *experiencing the pain of grief;*
3. *adjusting to life without the person who has died;*
4. *putting less emotional energy into grieving and putting it into something new – in other words, moving on.*

(NHS England, 2019a)

Your students will probably go through all of these stages but won't necessarily move smoothly from one to the next. Their grief may feel chaotic and out of control, but their feelings will eventually become less intense. Each bereavement is unique, and you can't tell how long it will last. For some the loss of a loved one will be at the forefront of their thoughts for a relatively short period of time whereas for others it can last for years. The NHS suggests that around 18 months is the average amount of time your students will be preoccupied with thoughts of their loved one.

In cases where there has been a bereavement it is advisable that the student should speak to their GP and look at engaging a counsellor through the NHS. Where this is difficult to arrange through the family, you might wish to consider gaining permission to explore this through your school nurse instead.

As a head of year, you will naturally be closely monitoring students who have suffered a bereavement and at times may feel that additional support is needed to help the student deal with their emotions. Some suitable support interventions could be art therapy, forest schools, sports activities or indeed anything that can allow the student space and time to be reflective while also providing a means to channel their thoughts and energy away from any outbursts.

Being available to talk and to listen to the student will also be of real benefit to them. Be careful not to attempt to fix all of their problems or try to protect them from everything (although you may do so in a subtle way with issues that are under your control). Instead you should listen to what the student has to say and allow them to work through their issues by expressing their thoughts and feelings to you in a trusted manner. Again, this is why building positive relationships with members of your year group is vital.

Acts of terrorism

Sadly, in the modern world students are aware of terrorist-related incidents and some unfortunately are caught up in acts of terrorism. Students who are caught up in terrorist incidents could experience one or more of the following common reactions to having been involved in the attack:

- *troubling thoughts, memories and mental imagery;*
- *disturbed sleep and/or nightmares;*
- *disturbed appetite, with either a marked increase or decrease in feeling hungry;*
- *sadness, despondency and apathy;*

- *irritability and anger;*
- *guilt and shame;*
- *emotional numbness;*
- *increased watchfulness or 'jumpiness';*
- *increased anxiety;*
- *poor concentration.*

(Manchester City Council, 2017)

Sometimes students who initially appear to be unaffected may experience difficulties many months after an event.

As a head of year you will most likely need to talk to your entire year group about an incident that has affected one of their peers, their local community or the wider country. It is important that when doing so you make it clear that the incident most likely has affected many children, families and communities. Work to reassure your students and also educate them on what they should do if they encounter a similar situation. Your local police force and even the government will often have clear advice for all people on what to do. Currently the advice is to 'run, hide, tell'.

Just like with other types of trauma, explore what support opportunities are available to your students and offer where you feel it is needed. When large-scale incidents happen such as terrorist attacks, there are often support packages created by the NHS, local police forces, local councils and the government which you can support families in accessing.

Being available to discuss issues with your students and having confidence that your students have a trusted adult in school with whom they can discuss their concerns is also very important.

Domestic violence

Some of your students may be a witness to domestic violence or even be in an abusive peer relationship. Regardless of whether they witness violence or are the victim, the impact on their lives can be serious even long after the threat of violence has passed (NHS England, 2019b).

Students who have witnessed or been subjected to domestic violence may exhibit some of the following symptoms. They may:

- *become anxious or depressed;*
- *have difficulty sleeping;*
- *have nightmares or flashbacks;*
- *complain of physical symptoms such as stomach aches;*
- *start to wet their bed;*
- *have temper tantrums;*
- *behave as though they are much younger than they are;*
- *display behavioural problems at school, or may start truanting;*
- *become aggressive;*

- *internalise their distress and withdraw from other people;*
- *have a lowered sense of self-worth;*
- *start to use alcohol or drugs;*
- *begin to self-harm by taking overdoses or cutting themselves;*
- *develop an eating disorder.*

(Women's Aid, 2011)

As a head of year you must report any suspected domestic violence issues to your school's designated safeguarding lead who will be able to advise you on how to proceed.

There are specific domestic abuse support organisations available that can provide trained staff to work with your students. It is advised that you find out where you can get support for your students before you actually need it. That way there will be no lost time between an issue becoming apparent and the beginning of support offered to your student.

School lock-down procedures

An increasing number of schools now have a lock-down procedure in place and some schools even practise these procedures in the same way they would a fire drill. Unfortunately, for a number of students, a practice lock-down can create a deep sense of stress within them.

Even where students are made aware that there is going to be a practice, the act of locking a classroom door, closing the blinds and asking everybody to huddle together in silence can create a stress response in students. Where there is pre-existing trauma there will always be an additional layer of risk in putting these students through a lock-down drill.

Unfortunately, for many schools the lock-down practice is here to stay and is a sad indictment of the world we find ourselves working in. With this in mind, you need to do more to support students during and immediately after a lock-down drill to manage its impact. Students should be given an opportunity to release after a lock-down drill.

One option is to tap into the 'flight' response and run a lap around the school field. If that is not possible, shaking, jumping or tapping are also possible options. The body uses these movements as ways to discharge the stress hormones released during the lock-down drill and it will help to limit the impact the lock-down has on your students.

Why consistency at school is key

Your students thrive in organised environments with routines and consistency. A well-managed and consistent school is important when dealing with students who have been through a trauma because it gives them a sense of security (Haynes, 2002).

At the point in time when you might be more tempted than ever to change the system in order to support your students, you must hold firm on the expectations that you have and the routines your school has in place. They offer a great sense of security, predictability and normalcy to what has been a tumultuous time in their lives. Should you begin to let up on some of your expectations because a student has been through a traumatic experience, one of the stable parts of their lives becomes less stable and less predictable and can lead to a spiral in terms of behaviour and well-being.

It can be very tempting to try and make things easier for your students when they go through difficult times. It is in their own interests for you to remain consistent in your approach.

Case study

Terrence was a head of year at a school in Greater Manchester. On 23 May 2017 he arrived at work to the news of a terrorist incident at a concert a number of his year group had been attending the night before.

He spoke with his tutor team before students began arriving and made sure everyone was aware of the events of the night before. He explained that a number of students had attended the concert and that it was important registers were completed quickly that morning so that he could see who wasn't in school and make contact with parents.

It was agreed that any students who had attended the concert would be monitored closely and support would be decided upon once a clearer picture of who had been present or had been in some way affected emerged.

Upon review of the registers, attendance calls were made and a number of students who were at the concert were identified. Of the four students identified as attending, three families chose to keep their children at home; only one was present in school. It wasn't until the subsequent days that it became more obvious that these students were isolating themselves from the rest of the student population. Terrence spoke to the students as a group but was unable to pinpoint any particular triggers within school other than the volume of people. He was mindful that the students needed consistency so did not offer to withdraw them from any lessons.

Terrence later spoke to parents and explained that the NHS was offering support to families affected and that the parents should discuss this with their GP. He explained that the students were isolating themselves from their peers and that he was worried that their response to the situation may worsen over time. All of the parents took Terrence's advice and were offered counselling support through the NHS.

The school provided a safe environment where the students could talk to key staff who they had identified as trusted adults. Over time, the group began to reintegrate with the rest of their peers.

The following year, the students were found by an English teacher, crying close to the student toilets. The school had created a memorial for the one-year anniversary of the incident but the students who were at the concert a year ago found it to be a reminder of events.

Rather than removing the memorial, Terrence acknowledged that they should have been consulted and then discussed with the students how they would like to remember those who had lost their lives and how this could be done more sensitively for people who attended. Involving the students in planning commemorative events allowed them to deal with their own grief, trauma and upset in a positive manner. Initially this hadn't happened at this school and it led to those who had already experienced trauma feeling upset by what the school had planned to be a positive gesture.

Summary

Being a head of year, you will be on the front line of supporting your students through some of the most difficult times of their teenage years. It is vitally important that you realise you will not have all of the answers and you will not be able to 'fix' anybody.

Trauma can affect people in any number of ways. Some of your students will appear as though nothing has happened while others will need support simply to set foot in the school building. Each case therefore will be unique and your approach should always take into account how the student is presenting to you.

Schools can inadvertently create trigger points for students who have already experienced trauma or even create new trauma for others. How you respond to 'stressful' scenarios and how you ensure your students can deal with situations they are placed in while at school should be a distinct area of focus for a head of year.

It isn't just the initial event that can cause trauma for your students. The following weeks, months or commemorative events each year can also cause them to relive and remember supressed thoughts and feelings about a traumatic event. You need to be mindful of this and where possible involve affected students in the planning of commemorations.

Finally, for many students experiencing trauma, schools are the most consistent and predictable part of their lives. You must ensure that in the face of wanting to support your students you do not allow the routines and expectations of school to slip. For some this additional change could be detrimental and lead to further stress.

1. What types of external support could you engage for your students when taking into consideration your specific context?

2. When dealing with a student going through a difficult time, how can you ensure you remain consistent?

3. How can you ensure everybody involved in supporting your year group is aware of the indicators of trauma?

4. How will you ensure positive student–teacher relationships are built with your year group?

References

Hall, P (2011) *Help Your Children Cope with Your Divorce: A Relate Guide.* London: Ebury Digital.

Haynes, F (2002) *The Ethical School: Consequences, Consistency and Caring.* Abingdon: Taylor & Francis.

Manchester City Council (2017) *Advice in Coping with the Anniversary.* [online] Available at: https://manchesterattacksupport.org.uk/advice-for-dealing-with-the-anniversary/ (accessed 9 March 2020).

NHS England (2019a) *Coping with Bereavement.* [online] Available at: www.nhs.uk/conditions/stress-anxiety-depression/coping-with-bereavement/ (accessed 9 March 2020).

NHS England (2019b) *Getting Help for Domestic Violence.* [online] Available at: www.nhs.uk/live-well/healthy-body/getting-help-for-domestic-violence/ (accessed 9 March 2020).

van der Kolk, B (2014) *The Body Keeps the Score: Mind, Brain and Body in the Transformation of Trauma.* London: Penguin.

Women's Aid (2011) *Meeting the Needs of Children Living with Domestic Violence in London.* London: NSPCC and Refuge.

II. WORKING TO DRIVE PROGRESS

What is progress?

You can be forgiven in the current educational context for thinking that progress is simply improving upon grades for your students. This is undoubtedly the focus for almost every school, where they are judged on what students achieve when they reach Year 11. Thankfully, in recent years there has been a shift in thinking to move away from simply increasing outcomes to the idea of students knowing more and remembering more (Harford, 2018).

It is important to remember that even with the shift in thinking, your primary source of information on how much progress your year group are making will be assessment data. It follows that where students know more and are able to remember more, their assessment scores should improve. As a head of year, you will have a unique viewpoint on how the numerous pastoral factors also contribute to a student's progress. It is this unique viewpoint of the whole student that means heads of year are well placed to support with driving progress.

Different progress measures

You will be expected to understand a number of key performance measures as a head of year, many of which you will have come across as a teacher even if you have no idea how they are generated. Likewise, when you first become a head of year it can be difficult to understand how these different measures provide you with an overall understanding of how your year group are performing.

I have included some of the main performance measures you will need to be aware of in this chapter, but it is worth mentioning that in most schools there are highly experienced and in some cases superhuman data managers and other admin staff who can support you in making sense of your performance data.

PROGRESS 8

Progress 8 is designed to look at the progress a pupil makes from the end of primary school to the end of secondary school. It compares each student's achievements with those of other pupils with similar prior attainment. A score of zero would indicate they have made progress which is, on average, the same as others with similar Key Stage 2 results. A negative number indicates they are behind statistically similar students and positive means they are doing better on average than those with similar Key Stage 2 results (Department for Education, 2016).

ATTAINMENT 8

Attainment 8 measures the achievement of a student across eight qualifications including maths and English, which are double weighted, three English Baccalaureate (EBacc) subjects and any three further qualifications. Attainment 8 will often be described in terms of 'buckets' and the focus is on how these buckets are filled (see Figure 11.1). The aim with Attainment 8 is to have a higher number as possible for each student. It is the Attainment 8 scores that are used to calculate Progress 8 scores so in that sense the two are linked together.

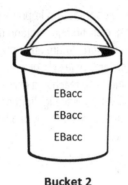

Bucket 1

One slot for English and one for mathematics. Both subjects are double weighted.

Bucket 2

Three EBacc subjects:
- sciences
- computer sciences
- geography
- history
- languages

Bucket 3

Three other slots that are made up of any remaining EBacc subjects, arts and vocational subjects.

Figure 11.1 Attainment 8 buckets

ASSESSMENT WITHOUT LEVELS

Originally intended only for use in national assessments, levels came to be used for in-school assessment between key stages in order to monitor whether students were on track to achieve expected levels at key points in their educational career.

Although this would appear to be a positive thing for a head of year attempting to analyse the progress of their year group, it was found that the use of levels distorted the purpose of in-school assessment, particularly day-to-day formative assessment. Often levels became viewed as thresholds and teaching became focused on getting pupils across the next threshold instead of ensuring they were secure in the knowledge and understanding defined in the programmes of study (Commission on Assessment without Levels, 2015).

More recently schools have moved away from using levels to measure progress throughout the year; often this is in favour of a series of colours or statements which indicate whether someone is achieving what they should at a particular time. For the head of year this means the need to fully understand your individual school's assessment and reporting methods becomes even more important. There is no longer a standardised system to fall back on and spotting progress can be more difficult across a cohort without the explicit use of levels or predictions.

How can a head of year improve progress?

It can be difficult as a head of year to see how you can improve progress and ultimately outcomes. Before thinking of unique progress strategies, first understand that the work you do around pastoral care, attendance and behaviour all impact upon future outcomes. You don't have the ability to influence departmental teaching across the whole school as a member of the senior leadership team would, nor can you direct departments to teach in a certain way like a head of department would. Instead your role in improving progress is to highlight areas of concern, ask uncomfortable questions of those who do have the influence of teaching and learning and finally to support students in being able to access their education.

ASSERTIVE MENTORING

Assertive mentoring is exactly what it says on the tin. All too often mentoring programmes with the right aims are created in schools but are used as a wholly supportive measure which can become 'woolly' in nature. When this happen the mentoring sessions can end up creating more excuses than solutions (SecEd, 2013).

With assertive mentoring the mentor sets clear targets that the student must achieve and the student must provide evidence of their achievement. For example, a student may be set the target of attending five revision sessions in a subject they are struggling in. At their next mentoring session they bring a signed attendance sheet demonstrating they have attended. The targets that are set need to clearly link to enabling the student to make progress but they also hold the student to account for their own achievement and progress in school.

CLEAR EXPECTATIONS

Having clear expectations cannot be underestimated. As a head of year you ultimately set the tone for your year group; what you expect of your students becomes the normal way of working. Your vision for your year group's achievement very quickly becomes the expectation, so you must make sure you expect the right things.

For some students it can feel right to expect less of them because they are struggling at home, have a SEND need or do not behave as you would expect. However, to accept these students should not do as well as others is to do them a disservice. Every student is able to achieve, some just need more support than others.

It would be equally easy to read this and decide you will expect every student to achieve the top grades. You must also be aware of how failing to meet expectations can have a negative impact upon your students. In reality it is a fine balancing act. It is always better to aim high and fall short rather than aiming for mediocrity.

PROVIDING INFORMATION FOR PARENTS AND CARERS

Parents and carers are a great support in helping to secure progress in students; however, schools can often be guilty of providing parents and carers with information they do not understand and not sharing what they can do to support students to make the progress they need to.

The information you provide to parents should be clear and simple to understand as parents often have preconceived ideas about schooling and individual subjects that can act as barriers to them supporting teachers. Making the information you provide accessible helps to remove these barriers. Making it clear how they can support students further removes barriers to parental engagement and ensures your students have support at home and in school.

Challenging conversations

When focusing on progress you will undoubtedly find yourself needing to hold challenging conversations with students, their families and colleagues. Nobody enjoys a conversation where you must be critical of another person. In the world of corporate business, challenging conversations aimed at making improvements are more common so it is useful to observe how these conversations are managed outside of education.

The following checklist is designed to help you prepare for a challenging conversation with a student, their family or a colleague with responsibility for an academic department.

- *Be direct*
- *Be specific*
- *Plan out the conversation*
- *Offer a solution*
- *Be empathetic*
- *Allow the other person to ask questions*

(Prossack, 2018)

It is important to remember that regardless of who the person you are speaking to is, a conversation about underperformance will be a personal one for them so avoid appearing cold or uninterested. You are there to get improvements for the student primarily; any other improvements should be seen as secondary to your goal of seeing an individual student make progress.

Case study

Lucinda analysed her year group's performance in their mock exams. The year group had performed well, with analysis tools predicting a Progress 8 score of +0.24. However, when looking at subject-level performance, Lucinda discovered that German had done significantly worse than all other subjects. On average students are achieving two grades lower than in any other subject area.

There were also a handful of students who despite having high prior attainment had significantly underperformed across a range of subjects. For some there were reasons that Lucinda was aware of – Charlotte, for example, had recently experienced a bereavement – but some of the students surprised Lucinda.

Lucinda scheduled a meeting with the head of languages to discuss her concerns. The conversation was direct but courteous. Lucinda explained to Don, the head of languages, that his subject was performing below the other curriculum areas and that she wanted to work with Don to help improve the results. Don was aware that his cohort had not performed well in the mocks but he explained to Lucinda that recent staffing changes had led to one class being very unsettled. Between them, they also identified a number of students who they should work closely with to monitor their effort in lessons and provide some catch-up work to complete at home.

The students who had performed below expectations across the school were placed onto a mentoring programme where they could be set targets every two weeks and supported in achieving their goals by a key member of staff.

Summary

Your role when driving progress is difficult to define. A head of year has a clear oversight of their group's performance across the whole school but limited input into the day-to-day teaching activities of teaching departments.

Despite this lack of direct involvement in teaching, you have influence over every other aspect of your students' school lives. Behaviour, attendance and other pastoral factors all contribute to how much progress students make at school. In this sense there is a wide variety of interventions you can put in place. What must be remembered, however, is that schools can become too focused on interventions; ultimately quality-first teaching is the best way to improve progress (Power, 2019). Because of this, the conversations you have with colleagues who manage departments will be just as important, if not more important, than your work tackling the peripheral issues of making progress.

❖ Reflections

1. How can you develop your understanding of progress measures?
2. What are your current areas for development for your year group?
3. How can you communicate this with staff responsible for teaching and learning?
4. How can you further support progress in your role as a head of year?

References

Commission on Assessment without Levels (2015) *Final Report of the Commission on Assessment without Levels.* London: UK Government.

Department for Education (2016) *Progress 8: How Progress 8 and Attainment 8 Measures Are Calculated.* London: Department for Education.

Harford, S (2018) *Ofsted Blog: Schools, Early Years, Further Education and Skills.* [online] Available at: https://educationinspection.blog.gov.uk/2018/04/23/assessment-what-are-inspectors-looking-at/ (accessed 9 March 2020).

Power, M (2019) *Ditch Interventions, Just Focus on Quality-First Teaching.* [online] Available at: www.tes.com/news/ditch-interventions-just-focus-quality-first-teaching (accessed 9 March 2020).

Prossack, A (2018) *How To Have Difficult Conversations At Work.* [online] Available at: www.forbes.com/sites/ashiraprossack1/2018/10/28/how-to-have-difficult-conversations-at-work/ (accessed 9 March 2020).

SecEd (2013) *Raising Attainment Using Data-driven 'Assertive' Mentoring.* [online] Available at: www.sec-ed.co.uk/best-practice/raising-attainment-using-data-driven-assertive-mentoring/ (accessed 9 March 2020).

12. TACKLING DISADVANTAGE

Identifying disadvantage

As a head of year you will be tasked with focusing on how certain vulnerable or disadvantaged groups are performing in relation to their peers. These will include those who are in receipt of free school meals, those on the SEND register and children who are looked after. However, in my experience, disadvantage can be transient. One-off events can create a vulnerability in the same way that long-term exposure to poverty can. Although the majority of this chapter is focused on identifying and supporting the different groups of disadvantaged students, you must also consider those who are disadvantaged but sit outside of the categories defined by your school or in this book.

PUPIL PREMIUM

The pupil premium is the standard measure for disadvantage that is used in schools. The term reflects the fact that for any student deemed to be 'pupil premium' there is an attached sum of money a school receives. To be categorised as pupil premium, a student would need to be in receipt of free school meals now or at any time in the past six years (House of Commons Committee of Public Accounts, 2013).

As with most indicators of disadvantage, the pupil premium measure only identifies students where they have been in receipt of free school meals. Not all students who could have applied for free school meals will apply. Likewise, families where income may be slightly above the threshold for free school meals may also have higher outgoings, leading to the family living in relative poverty. Although schools use the pupil premium as their main identifier of disadvantaged students and are judged according to how much progress pupil premium students make, there are many other disadvantaged groups that do not receive the same level of attention. As a head of year you must advocate for all students who are disadvantaged, not just those who are easiest to detect.

BLACK, ASIAN AND MINORITY ETHNIC GROUPS

The Department for Education highlights each year how black (and white) students perform worse than Chinese, Asian and mixed ethnic groups. Students from a traveller or Roma background perform even lower (Department for Education, 2019). Yet it is common in educational discourse to focus on black, Asian and minority ethnic (BAME) students and white students separately. This could have the effect of hiding the underperformance of black students or reducing the BAME groups' outcomes for your school, again hiding the true picture.

To look at your year group in terms of BAME students you will need to be more nuanced, focusing on individual students or smaller subgroups of your cohort. It is important that you don't simply assume there is no disadvantage to being a BAME student within your school. Not every student will experience their education in the same way you did or their peers do (Eddo-Lodge, 2017).

The reality is that a lower proportion of black students choose to go on to further study than other ethnic groups (Fazackerley, 2019) and part of addressing this issue within your year group must be concerned with improving the aspirations of these students so they are able to perform as well as their peers and have expectations in-line with these outcomes.

LOOKED AFTER CHILDREN

A looked after child is a student who has been in the care of the local authority for more than 24 hours. Looked after children may be living:

- with foster parents;
- in a residential children's home;
- in residential settings like schools or secure units.

Looked after children are no less able than their peers but often underachieve. This can be due to missed schooling when first entering the care system or where placements break down, and they are also more likely to be excluded from school due to displaying challenging behaviour or persistently failing to follow the school rules.

Other reasons for underachievement include the damaging experiences they may have had prior to entering care, the lack of co-ordinated educational support or, most prevalent, low expectations for them (Department for Education and Skills, 2006). Low expectations can be from the student's care placement or from the school itself. It is important that you as a head of year are clear that any students who are looked after are expected to achieve the same as any other student.

SPECIAL EDUCATIONAL NEEDS AND DISABILITY (SEND)

Students who are categorised as having a special educational need or disability should have a plan in place to support them in their schooling from your school's SEND department. The area of SEND can be complicated and your school's SEND co-ordinator should be able to support you in your work with tacking disadvantage in this area.

Although your school will have a SEND co-ordinator, as a head of year you share responsibility for ensuring that your SEND students make progress and for their pastoral care. The key is to work collaboratively and to draw upon the expertise of your colleagues. Being a head of year involves bringing together many different departments within a school for the benefit of your year group.

Tackling disadvantage

Once you have an understanding of some ways your students could be disadvantaged, you need to work out how best to support these students and tackle disadvantage. Based on research completed by the Department for Education, Figure 12.1 highlights areas a head of year can work on to tackle disadvantage within your year group (Sharp et al, 2015).

Figure 12.1 Tackling disadvantage

QUALITY-FIRST TEACHING

Quality-first teaching should be at the heart of tackling disadvantage. All students deserve access to the very best teaching. Although a head of year doesn't have direct influence on the teaching of lessons, your insight into what is occurring around the school is invaluable in helping to improve the quality of teaching for your year group.

This can be achieved by either directly sharing strategies for improving teaching for individual students or sharing your observations with department leaders to help bring about improvements in teaching. Quite simply if your students are being taught well they are more likely to succeed.

BEHAVIOUR AND ATTENDANCE

As seen in Chapter 4, managing behaviour within your year group is key to helping students to engage with their education. Likewise, students can only engage with their education if they are attending school. When focusing on tackling any perceived disadvantage it is of the utmost importance that all students are expected to achieve the same with regards to behaviour and attendance.

Monitoring behaviour and attendance can also support you in identifying where there are potential issues for your disadvantaged students. For example, an increase in behavioural issues could be an indication of increased stress at home.

MEETING INDIVIDUAL NEEDS

Although consistency in approach and having the same high expectations of all your students is important in tackling disadvantage, you must also take account of the needs of individual students and work with them to overcome any barriers to learning. In the classroom this would be called differentiation, but it should take into account more than just learning needs. Some of your students will need supporting out of class to ensure that they have eaten, to provide support for a bereavement or to engage in extra-curricular activities.

It is impossible to list the multiple avenues of support that could be provided for a student and sometimes having a 'tick list' of interventions is unhelpful. Understanding what each disadvantaged student needs in order to engage in their education is what will make a difference.

RESPONDING TO DATA

There are vast amounts of data created by schools around behaviour, attendance and even the meals eaten on a particular day. It can be easy to find this overwhelming, yet when looking at disadvantaged students it can provide a good oversight of where your year group's issues are and can also provide an early warning of issues before they manifest in larger ways or underperformance.

A dip in attendance or spike in poor behaviour can be an indicator of a student experiencing difficulties at home; a student missing meals can be an early indicator of a child experiencing poverty. Likewise a dip in homework grades or being late for certain lessons can indicate more school-specific issues that you can support a student with, such as issues with a particular subject or teacher.

Although data can provide a great insight into your year group and the potential issues your vulnerable students may be facing, it can sometimes produce outliers where, for example, there is an increase in lateness but this is due to the student having new friends who live further away from school who walk together. Outliers don't fit what you would expect to see from a particular student and could lead you down a rabbit hole where no issues exist at all. Particularly when looking at academic data, sometimes students can have a bad day which isn't representative of their usual performance levels.

STRONG LEADERSHIP

Strong leadership is needed when focusing on disadvantaged students because often the issues being faced are severe and these pupils are deserving of as much help as possible. Without a strong leader the systems put in place to tackle disadvantage will amount to very little. Being a strong leader allows you to set a clear vision, communicate effectively to colleagues and influence real results.

The clear vision gives your colleagues a better understanding of direction and makes their roles and responsibilities clear. Unlike a manager, a leader not only sets the tone for work with disadvantaged students but models how best to work with them, guides colleagues in their work and supports both staff and students in maximising the achievement for disadvantaged students.

ETHOS

Overall, the ethos you create around tackling disadvantage will be the decisive factor. When you work in a school where it is expected that all students will be supported in achieving their goals and no disadvantaged students are left behind, it is more likely to actually happen. Although much of this chapter discusses how some adaptations need to be made in your practice to ensure disadvantaged students can succeed, it is important to not expect less of them. Nothing will do more damage to the prospects of a disadvantaged student that expecting them to do less well than their peers.

Engaging families

One key way you can support more disadvantaged students is to engage with their families and caregivers. Schools are an integral part of any community. As a head of year, you need to take a central role in fostering relationships between the school and the wider community (Hewitt-Clarkson, 2017). Being knowledgeable about the local community will allow you to understand emergent issues for your year group's disadvantaged students. Being engaged with the community means engaging directly with the families of your students, particularly those who are disadvantaged.

However, all of this work relies on trust between you and the community. This can be a fragile thing to maintain and nurture, but the overall impact upon your most disadvantaged students will be immeasurable. Many families don't like to be judged by an outsider and will feel that your work does just that, so building up these relationships allows you to challenge the support structure for your disadvantaged students without causing upset and anxiety. Done correctly, engaging the families of your disadvantaged students should be the embodiment of your overall ethos. When the community know you are there to support them, they are more likely to be open and honest about the challenges they are facing and allow you to provide the required help.

Case study

Lucy, head of Year 10, noticed a pattern in the behaviour of one of her pupil premium cohort, Amelia, who appeared to have more behavioural issues later in the school day. Initially Lucy discussed this with Amelia's teachers. Although they could all see the pattern, none of them had any ideas on why it was the case. After looking at more of her students, Lucy noticed that the same was true of a number of other children and so decided to speak to each student individually.

The conversations were all very different. All of the students were entitled to a free school meal and so Lucy did not question their eating habits at all. However, in a conversation with a parent later in the week, Lucy discovered that a number of students had been sharing lunches with their peers. Lucy decided to discuss this with the catering manager at school, who could look at what each student bought every day.

Lucy identified that a number of students who were entitled to free school meals were spending their money at breakfast time when they arrived at school, often meaning they had little money left to purchase a dinner. These were the same students who were displaying more challenging or defiant behaviour later in the school day.

From this, Lucy worked with her line manager to fund a breakfast club where students could have toast and juice each morning for free. After several weeks Lucy reanalysed her behaviour reports and found that incidents from the students who were now receiving a breakfast had decreased and that they were now buying a full meal at lunchtimes with their school meal allowance.

Lucy continued to investigate any further issues facing her disadvantaged students and worked tirelessly to make sure that all teachers of her year group expected the same for every student, regardless of whether they are classed as being disadvantaged or not.

Summary

It is easy to become overwhelmed with the task of supporting your disadvantaged students. It speaks to the very heart of the human condition, wanting to support those who are in need to ensure they can make a success of their lives in the future but not always being able to identify what the actual cause of their disadvantage is, let alone knowing how to solve any issues.

It is easy to assume that everybody has a similar understanding of what success and progress look like. When you fail to take the time to understand what these are for your students you can be at risk of becoming oppressive in your practice. Not everybody aspires to a university education, for example, so forcing this view on your students can lead to some feeling that they don't fit in. This isn't to say you don't think some of your students can achieve this, just that some may not see this as their goal in life. Bear this in mind whenever you discuss or make decisions surrounding your work with disadvantaged students.

Data is a tool that can support you in understanding the needs of your disadvantaged students but it does not give you the full picture. Each student is a living, breathing and thinking individual and their experiences are equally if not more important than any data that can be produced about them. There are also colleagues within your school who will have a better knowledge and understanding of different sets of data. Your job isn't to become a master of all the data available but to call upon the necessary expertise to help you build a bigger picture of the disadvantaged students in your year group.

❖ Reflections

1. How are different groups of students in your year group disadvantaged?
2. What systems are in place or could be put in place to allow you to monitor data for your disadvantaged students?
3. What is your vision for disadvantaged students in your year group?
4. How will you ensure your vision is carried out by colleagues within your school?

References

Department for Education (2019) *GCSE Results ('Attainment 8')*. London: Department for Education.

Department for Education and Skills (2006) *Supporting Looked After Learners*. Nottingham: DfES Publications.

Eddo-Lodge, R (2017) *Why I'm No Longer Talking to White People about Race*. London: Bloomsbury.

Fazackerley, A (2019) *'Look at How White the Academy Is': Why BAME Students Aren't Doing PhDs*. [online] Available at: www.theguardian.com/education/2019/sep/12/look-at-how-white-the-academy-is-why-bame-students-arent-doing-phds (accessed 9 March 2020).

Hewitt-Clarkson, S (2017) Community Cohesion and Social Integration. In First, T (ed) *Challenging Disadvantage Together* (pp 22-5). London: Teach First.

House of Commons Committee of Public Accounts (2013) *Early Action: Landscape Review*. London: Stationery Office.

Sharp, C, Macleod, S, Bernardinelli, D, Skipp, A and Higgins, S (2015) *Supporting the Attainment of Disadvantaged Pupils*. London: Department for Education.

13. PARENTAL ENGAGEMENT

Communicating with parents and carers

As a head of year, you are likely to be speaking to parents and carers daily regarding any number of issues or events at school. Your communication will be varied, from letters home and phone calls to formal meetings and information events, from impersonal whole year group communications to communication specifically about an individual student and their needs.

It can be easy to fall into the trap of only communicating with parents and carers when a student does something wrong. Although it is right for you to be making contact during these times, for many parents and carers this will be the first time they have spoken directly with you about their child. Consider carefully how you communicate your message, as you should be aiming not only to deal with the emergent issue but also to build a relationship with those who care for your student in order to support both student and family in the future. As much as possible you should aim to make contact with parents and carers early in the year to share positives or even simply to introduce yourself.

TOP TIPS FOR COMMUNICATION

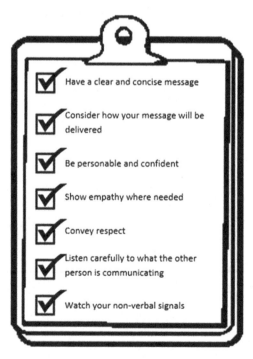

Figure 13.1 Checklist for communication with parents and carers

First impressions matter and will leave a lasting impression. Be aware of how you present yourself and ensure you communicate that you are there to support rather than criticise. If the first impression is that parents and carers feel criticised it can lead to the overall message being lost and both parties feeling unhappy and issues remaining unresolved.

A quick communication checklist

One of your main goals when communicating with parents and carers should be to build trust between them and the school. It is often useful to view any communication from the point of view of the student's family. You are asking them to trust you with one of their most precious things, their child, therefore you should not be surprised when parents or carers become emotional or even combative during your communications with them. What you must demonstrate is that you are working in the best interests of the student and are therefore on the same side (Power, 2019).

ENGAGING THOSE WHO DON'T ENGAGE

Some parents and carers are naturally more difficult to engage in school matters. They may be difficult to contact on the phone or never attend a parents' evening. In these situations, it is vital that you think carefully about how you will deliver your messages.

Some parents and carers work shift patterns that make it difficult for them to answer phone calls during the school day, others are suspicious of a withheld phone number and some have simply grown tired of being called for behavioural issues by different teachers from school.

First, you should discuss with the student at school how best to contact home. Often this will reveal that a phone number has been changed or that messages are being listened to on voicemails, just not responded to.

Second, you need to set up a line of communication, either via a phone call, email, letter or even by completing a home visit. From this initial line of communication, you can explain the importance of being able to contact home in an emergency and also discuss what communications the parents and carers would find useful to receive. If you agree a plan for communication with a family it is important that this is then communicated to anybody within your school who might need to know, including teachers and administrative staff.

On a broader scale you should think carefully about what types of communication parents and carers are receiving from school and how these messages are communicated. Is everything sent home with students as a letter when some may never make it out of a school bag or is everything sent via text message so that parents are inundated with messages on their phone? There must be an understanding of just how much information you are expecting parents to receive and how this is best communicated.

Handling complaints

Your school will have a complaints procedure for parents, carers and members of the community to use. It sets out who they should contact and how their complaint will be dealt with. In reality, a number of complaints will first come to the school through you as a head of year. For many parents you are the first port of call and having built up a positive relationship with the family you find they are looking to you to resolve their issue.

Listening fully to the concerns being raised is the most important step in addressing any complaint. Whether the complaint is made to you in person, in writing or over the phone, it is important that you make notes of what exactly the person is unhappy about and clarify that this is in fact the case with them. Not only does it demonstrate you have listened to them, it ensures you are dealing with the issue and not focusing on the wrong thing. It is often useful to ask the person making a complaint how they would like the issue to be resolved and where reasonable try to reach this goal.

You need to ensure you make a record of any investigation that takes place and also any remedial action. Once you have all of the facts of an incident in order, relay them back to the person making the complaint clearly and concisely before saying how an issue has been resolved. You should always try to agree a timeframe with the person making a complaint and then stick to it.

These steps not only resolve a complaint, they also help to build trust. You should always remember the checklist for any communication with parents and carers given in Figure 13.1.

HANDLING COMPLAINTS ABOUT YOURSELF

It is inevitable that you will eventually have to handle a complaint that is about yourself, where a parent or carer feels that you have acted in a way that has prejudiced their child. As someone who is expected to manage the behaviour of a year group these instances become more likely.

Having someone directly challenge the work you have done or the actions you have taken will elicit an emotional response. It is important in these scenarios to remember the conflict resolution model looked at in Chapter 2. The PIN model, originally developed by Andrew Acland (1990), helps you to understand what issue is being presented by the person making a complaint, before moving to a position where both parties acknowledge that the needs of the students are central to any discussions and that the emotional response from either side of this perceived conflict is because of this shared interest.

Just as with any other complaint, it is important that you listen to the person and acknowledge that their thoughts on a scenario are being considered. Keep clear records of any investigations that take place and offer the option of another member of staff to deal with the situation should the person making a complaint feel it necessary. Ultimately, if the issue is about a member of staff, parents and carers can follow the school's complaints procedure.

Candour with parents

Candour is essentially being open and honest. The idea of being honest with parents shouldn't be anything new to you. However, there are times when, without realising it, you may not be as open as you can be about a student causing you concern or where a sanction needs to be put in place.

We naturally try to avoid difficult conversations with people. Although it is polite to leave a voicemail explaining who called, you should avoid leaving one that goes into too much detail about the issue that has occurred, any sanctions that are to be served and decisions made (Patterson et al, 2012). It is important that you have communicated an issue directly with parents or carers rather than allowing them to find out from a recorded message.

Not only does this build up trust between the families and school, it ensures there is no misunderstanding over what the message is. It also provides parents and carers with a chance to discuss what you are saying to them. Sometimes this will lead to you, as the person speaking with them, being challenged on a decision, which is why before communicating with any parents or carers you should have a clear message. This involves being acquainted with all the facts of an issue and being confident in providing the solution to the problem.

Occasionally there will be issues between staff and students. Sometimes it is the case that you and other teachers will get things wrong; for example, sanctioning the wrong student or marking an assessment wrong. However tempting it may be to let these mistakes slip by, to maintain the trust between you and the family or the school and the family you should always explain to parents and carers any incidents involving their child where you got it wrong. This is difficult to begin with, but it allows for a positive relationship to be built which is a good foundation for any future issues.

Public speaking

There are times as a head of year where you will need to engage with the parents and carers of students in your year group as a whole at information events or presentations. Speaking to a room filled with adults feels very different from addressing your weekly year group assembly, and for some this can be a nerve-wracking ordeal.

Most fears about public speaking are rooted in irrational beliefs (Ellis and Dryden, 1987), which make you feel that speaking at an event is in some way dangerous or harmful when in reality it is neither. What you are most likely afraid of is being judged by the parents and carers with whom you have worked to build up a relationship and not delivering your message clearly.

The same rules apply in public speaking as they do in any form of communication with parents and carers, but particular focus needs to be placed on appearing confident yet personable and having a clear and concise message. Planning what you are going to say is key. Make sure you give your audience all of the information that they need in digestible chunks – it is very much like planning a lesson. You must always remember that many parents and carers will be coming to you following a busy day, so keeping your message concise is almost always a crowd-pleaser and allows you more time for one-to-one discussions with families at the end.

Case study

Fidan was new to the role of head of Year 9 in January. The year group had previously been led by two other heads of year who had moved on to different roles. One of the first things Fidan noticed when she was contacting parents about behavioural issues was that parents were often dismissive of what she was saying, were argumentative or simply ignored her phone calls.

Prior to Fidan taking up her role, communication with parents and carers had been minimal. Some parents complained to Fidan that they had attempted to contact teachers on numerous occasions and had simply been ignored.

When Fidan had conversations with parents and carers regarding behaviour she found that her phone call was often the first they had heard of any issues. This led to conflict with some, as Fidan couldn't say exactly what was happening when the incident occurred, only what information had been passed to her.

Fidan created a plan that involved requesting that any students who had been entered into detention or removed from a classroom should receive a phone call home from the classroom teacher within 24 hours. The teacher should then update the behaviour incident log to show they had either called home or left a voicemail. This was then monitored by Fidan and immediately increased the communication from other members of staff with parents.

Second, Fidan intended to tackle her parents' evening attendance, which had been notoriously low for the past two years. She sent a letter home inviting parents and carers to parents' evening but also included a reply slip. If people did not reply, pastoral and admin staff called home to find out if they would be attending. Following the parents' evening anybody who didn't attend was again contacted and asked what could be done to help them attend the next event.

Finally Fidan decided to create a year group newsletter that would go out to parents via email or be printed for those without an email address. It contained good news stories about the year group, important dates coming up in the school year and any other messages she needed to communicate about school life for the students.

Over time Fidan found parents and carers were more willing to engage in phone calls about behaviour because they understood any previous issues that had taken place within the classroom. Attendance at parents' evenings increased and the feedback Fidan received from parents and carers was positive, with one parent commenting that she loved knowing exactly what had been happening in school through the newsletter.

Summary

It is easy for teachers of any seniority to see making phone calls as an administrative task that takes time away from other important matters. You must make the case strongly that timely communication with parents not only will help to improve behaviour, it will allow the parents and carers to support the school and feel that they are being involved in their child's education.

As with any type of communication, it is important that you consider using the best medium possible to send out your message. It would never be appropriate to send out an urgent message via second-class post so plan ahead – not just what you will say but how this will be communicated.

You must remember that to many parents, carers and indeed students, you are the first point of contact from school, which means inevitably you will be the first point of contact for complaints. Note that some complaints are subject to specific processes that sit outside of your school's complaints procedure, such as when dealing with exclusions (Department for Education, 2019). Nevertheless you should be able to explain to those who contact you how they can progress their complaint to the correct person or authority.

All of your work around parental engagement is ultimately about building positive relationships between school and home. You are in a good position within the school to effect change in this area and it can have wide-reaching consequences for your students' time at school.

❖ Reflections

1. What messages do you give to parents and carers when you communicate with them?

2. How will you work to engage parents and carers who are difficult to communicate with?

3. Are there steps you can take to ensure that you have built positive relationships with parents and carers prior to any issues arising?

4. What steps will you take to ensure you can communicate publicly with the parents and carers of your students?

5. How can you build trust with parents and carers?

References

Acland, A F (1990) *A Sudden Outbreak of Common Sense: Managing Conflict Through Mediation.* London: Random House Business Books.

Department for Education (2019) *Best Proactive Guidance for School Complaints Procedures 2019.* London: Department for Education.

Ellis, A and Dryden, W (1987) *The Practice of Rational-Emotive Therapy (RET).* New York: Springer Publishing Company.

Patterson, K, Grenny, J, McMillan, R, and Switzler, A (2012) *Crucial Conversations: Tools for Talking When Stakes Are High.* London: McGraw-Hill.

Power, M (2019) What They Didn't Teach Me about Building Trust with Parents. In Mullin, S (ed) *What They Didn't Teach Me on My PGCE* (pp 39–40). Ontario: Word and Deed Publishing Incorporated.

14. LEADING FROM THE MIDDLE

Middle leadership

In its simplest form, middle leadership within a secondary school is the level between classroom teachers and the senior leadership team. This can be as a subject leader, leading a school priority area, as a SENCO or literacy leader, or – for you – as a head of year. All middle leadership roles are vital in securing the best outcomes for students.

As a head of year, your responsibilities overlap with every other middle leader within the school, because while each person focuses on individual aspects of a student's schooling, your job is to bring all of this together and look at the whole student.

In general, middle leaders are accountable to line managers for the quality of the work in their area of responsibility (Glover et al, 1999). There is a managerial expectation that you will monitor your colleagues' work (Wise, 2003). While that expectation is recognised by middle leaders as one of their responsibilities, many are reluctant to hold members of their team accountable for their practice (Bennett et al, 2007). Instead many middle leaders see their role more as a position to motivate, support and develop staff; there is therefore a real tension between being part of a team yet also attempting to manage that same team.

A middle leader possesses a formal responsibility for an area of the school's work, yet to be effective in your role your formal position should not be the basis of your authority. Many successful middle leaders possess little formal authority, relying instead on their relationships with members of the department (Wettersten, 1994).

Middle leadership is difficult. You not only have a leadership responsibility but also a substantial teaching commitment which you must try and balance. At times this can present some real challenges to your workload and ability to get work done. It may often feel like you are stuck in the middle, not leading from the middle!

The head of year and leadership

Although there are many books about middle leadership, there are far fewer about being a head of year. Unlike leading a curriculum area, being a head of year means you not only want students to perform well in their subjects but you also need to provide support mechanisms for pastoral issues and opportunities for students to develop themselves in ways that are not limited by a subject.

Although there are measurable outcomes, such as attendance and behaviour, many areas of your work will be much harder to measure, which in turn can make it more difficult to manage your team of tutors and other staff in how they should be working with your year group. Where a head of department would have lesson observations and work scrutiny at their disposal to judge the effectiveness of their teams, you will need to use a different set of tools such as student voice, reviewing interventions and observing a tutor time session. However, one of the most effective ways to monitor and support what is occurring with your team is to create a culture of reflective practice, where you share good practice and support one another to embed it across the year group.

The pressure to scrutinise is ever-present in any middle leadership role. You must be careful not to reduce the pastoral activities of your team to something that can be seen in a short ten-minute direct observation or recorded on a tick sheet to say an intervention was completed. You can, of course, observe the quality of tutor time delivery and spot check that rules have been enforced, but the work that has the biggest impact, building relationships, working with families and making real changes to the lives of students, isn't so easy to measure.

Managing up and down

As a middle leader you are not only accountable to your line manager and the senior leadership team, you are also accountable to the staff that you lead. Being able to manage both of these will take time to master (Lewis, 2018).

Your team will require direction in order to fulfil the necessary tasks and make advances towards your vision of progress. But you will also need to spend time ensuring members of the senior leadership team are kept fully informed, managing their expectations and meeting their priorities, while your students are given the appropriate challenge or support. At times this can be as simple as asking a member of your senior leadership team to engage with a family if you have exhausted other options, but it might also include being an advocate for your students when decisions are being made.

At times, the senior leadership team will make demands regarding students in your year group that you might disagree with. Your job in these situations isn't simply to follow instructions. You must advocate for what is best for your students. It won't always be an easy discussion to have but your role provides you with a good knowledge of each member of your year group and sometimes this knowledge provides a different insight into a situation; you must share this insight and influence decisions.

REFLECTIVE PRACTICE

Most teachers will have encountered reflective practice at some point and teachers are inherently reflective. Understanding what worked and what didn't in a lesson before making changes is a key example of this. To help you develop your own practice, but also to allow your team to share with you some of the trials and tribulations of their work, creating a culture of reflecting upon practice is vital. This could be as simple as a conversation once every two weeks to discuss key work with your students, or even a reflective log of work done with key students which can help you and those you lead to understand what is being done and how it can be improved.

Reflective practice within your team can take place in a number of ways such as:

- team meetings;
- one-on-one coaching sessions;
- a reflective log;
- observing the practice of others;
- meetings with key teaching staff for students;
- pupil and staff voice activities.

Being a strong middle leader

Middle leaders are often referred to as the *'engine room'* of a school (Margetts, 2018) and there is good reason for this. Not only do you hold responsibility and accountability for a year group, you are in control of putting into action many of the changes required to bring about improvements with your year group and team of tutors. To be a strong middle leader you need to have the capacity to know your vision (covered in Chapter 15) and then empower your team to work towards shared goals.

Your role has the potential to drive a great deal of change within your school as well as managing the day-to-day work of a team of tutors. Teachers, on the whole, come to the profession to share a passion for their subject. The pastoral work expected of most teachers in their role as a tutor can often be viewed as less important or be the area where teachers struggle to understand fully their roles and responsibilities.

As a strong middle leader you will need to support your team in managing the potential conflicts between teaching and being a tutor and also work to develop your team to deliver top quality pastoral intervention. This will require not only management and holding your team to account over issues but developing their skills through coaching, training sessions and team meetings where strategies can be shared.

Case study

When writing her year group improvement plan, Evangeline was able to outline her team's journey for the coming year. Within this plan, Evangeline made sure there was: change; high expectations; supportive and rigorous processes and protocols that also hold staff to account; and opportunities to delegate and empower.

Evangeline was passionate about developing her team, particularly the new members of staff. She wanted to ensure that the students in her year group were provided with the highest quality PSHE curriculum delivery within tutor time each week while still ensuring enough time was given to monitoring the standards of uniform and equipment each day before lessons.

Because two of the new members of staff were newly qualified teachers, Evangeline decided that the best way to develop their tutor time practice was to merge the two groups together when they were to be taught PSHE and to deliver the sessions herself with the two tutors supporting her with parts of the delivery.

Over time the tutors built up a positive relationship with one another and with Evangeline, with whom they worked closely each week. Their understanding of how Evangeline wanted the sessions to be delivered became clear and, although they sometimes struggled with the content, they knew Evangeline was available to support them. After a number of weeks of teaching in this way, each of the tutors began to take it in turns to lead a session with Evangeline and the other tutor still present as support.

Not only was Evangeline building up relationships with her tutors through doing this, she was able to model what good practice looked like and help her team to develop their skills properly before being expected to deliver sessions on their own. Long term, this meant that the quality of PSHE provision within Evangeline's year group was high and she could allow her team to continue delivering content without so much input from her.

Summary

Relationships are at the heart of the work you do as a leader. As with your students, when you want to bring about change and develop other people you need to build up positive relationships with them first so that you can challenge them when it is needed and trust them to deliver your vision and goals.

In the case study Evangeline not only built up positive relationships with members of her team, she also increased her own credibility. Equally important is your ability to demonstrate the skills you want to develop in others as this is often the best way to teach others what it is you are looking for.

Your leadership role will at times lead to situations where you need to push back against decisions being made because you don't believe they will be beneficial to your students. It is vital that you take on these situations fully to advocate for your year group. This in itself is great leadership, informed by your own values and moral purpose.

❖ Reflections

1. How does the head of year role fit within your school's structure?

2. How will you balance your teaching commitments with your pastoral role and then maintain that balance?

3. How will you reflect upon the practice of you and your team and use that to make improvements?

4. What strategies could you use to deal with senior leaders when you disagree with the decision they are making about your students?

References

Bennett, N, Woods, P, Wise, C, and Newton, W (2007) Understandings of Middle Leadership in Secondary Schools: A Review of Empirical Research. *School Leadership and Management*, 27(5): 453–70.

Glover, D, Miller, D, Gambling, M, Gough, G and Johnson, M (1999) As Others See Us: Senior Management and Subject Staff Perceptions of the Work Effectiveness of Subject Leaders in Secondary Schools. *School Leadership and Management*, 19(3): 331–45.

Lewis, D-M (2018) *Is Middle Leadership For You?* [online] Available at: www.teachertoolkit.co.uk/2018/03/26/middle-leader-move/ (accessed 9 March 2020).

Margetts, S (2018) *Focus On Developing Senior and Middle Leaders*. [online] Available at: www.leadershipmatters.org.uk/articles/focus-upon-developing-the-senior-and-middle-leaders/ (accessed 9 March 2020).

Wettersten, J (1994) *Low Profile, High Impact: Four Case Studies of High School Department Chairs Whose Transactions Transform Teachers and Administrators.* New Orleans, LA: Annual Meeting of the American Educational Research Association.

Wise, C (2003) Leaders of Subject Communities. In Bennett, N and Anderson, L (eds) *Rethinking Educational Leadership* (pp 131–42). London: Sage Publications.

15. VISION AND ETHOS

What is vision?

Your vision is simply what you want to achieve for your pupils and team, usually in the form of a goal or goals that are distinctive to your team and your year group. Your vision in this sense is the overarching aim; the most aspirational outcome for your time with your year group. Your goals provide the stepping stones to achieving your overall vision and are usually measurable. Once you have a vision it becomes important for this to be shared with and by those with whom you work. The trick, according to Andy Buck (2017), is to create a vision that distinguishes you from other year groups and other schools. Your year group is unique and your vision for them should be just as unique.

Dreaming is the first step in creating your vision. You shouldn't be afraid to dream big; you can always scale down your vision to meet the realities of the context at a later point. This allows you to think about ideas that may not seem likely in the current situation but long term, through strategic planning, could indeed become possible. For example, you could aspire for all students in your year group to leave school with the skills necessary for the modern workforce. Within the traditional curriculum this might be difficult to achieve, therefore you need to provide opportunities for your students to experience new technologies.

Developing a vision

A vision is a great tool in any leadership position, but you need to be able to develop a vision that is specific for your context and your own year group. There are six building blocks that fit within the two key elements of any good vision statement (see Figure 15.1). For your vision to work it must both be inspirational and offer stability to your team and students. Once this is in place it will provide a foundation for your year group and team of tutors to work from (Institute of Action Research for Community Health, 2012).

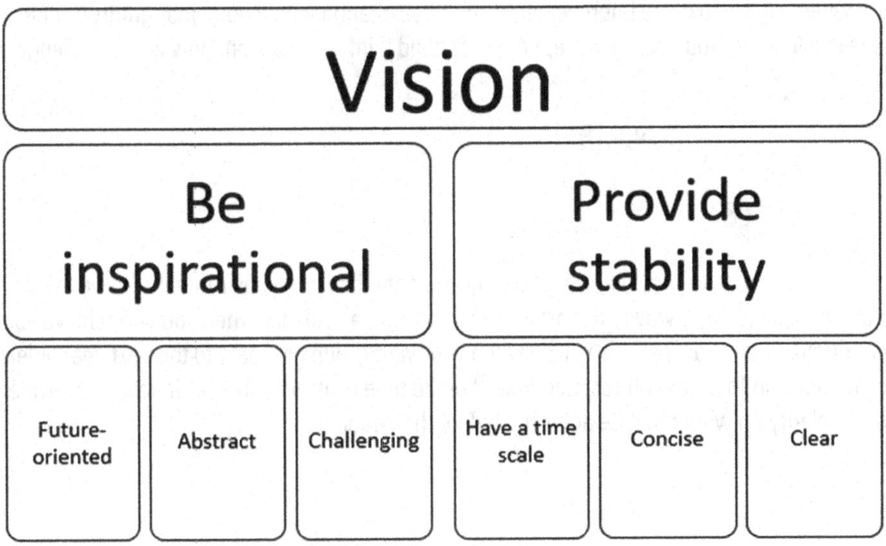

```
┌─────────────────────────────────────────────────────────┐
│                        Vision                             │
└─────────────────────────────────────────────────────────┘
┌──────────────────────────┐  ┌──────────────────────────┐
│           Be             │  │         Provide          │
│      inspirational       │  │        stability         │
└──────────────────────────┘  └──────────────────────────┘
┌────────┐┌────────┐┌──────────┐┌──────────┐┌────────┐┌────────┐
│Future- ││Abstract││Challenging││Have a time││Concise ││ Clear  │
│oriented││        ││          ││  scale   ││        ││        │
└────────┘└────────┘└──────────┘└──────────┘└────────┘└────────┘
```

Figure 15.1 Building blocks of vision

AN INSPIRATIONAL VISION

future-oriented

Your vision statement is ultimately your goals for your year group. Improvement is a long-term process and there is always more to do. With that in mind, your vision must be future-oriented and ultimately focus on your students' lives after school; however, they may change depending on where in their educational journey your year group are. A vision in Year 7 might be completely different to the vision of a Year 11 cohort. What is it you are trying to achieve to support them in their next steps?

Abstract

Being abstract is really important because often your vision can be limited by what you know happens currently or what you know students typically go on to do from your school. When creating a vision, it is time to think beyond this. Think about all of the possibilities that are out there for your students and what you can do in order to help them reach beyond their predecessors.

Challenging

Your vision must challenge you, your team and your students. If it doesn't it becomes simply a statement of fact or a note on what it is you currently do. Your vision statement is what you refer back to when you try to make improvements and drive change within your year group. Getting better is challenging. You need to accept this and build it into your vision. How will it challenge you?

A VISION TO PROVIDE STABILITY

Have a time scale

Your vision also needs to provide some much-needed stability in an environment where things can often change quickly. One way to do this is to provide a time scale for when you will achieve your vision. For most heads of year this will be when your year group graduate to the next year or leave school to move on to new ventures. Regardless of the time scale you choose, it helps to provide focus and clarity on what must be achieved before the deadline.

Concise

Often when a vision statement is created, either the words are too generic or the statement turns into a long wish list of things you would like to achieve. The vision you have must be realistic and sufficiently concise to be shared easily with your students and team of tutors. It should be easy to refer back to and the overall goal should be crystal clear. Without this your vision can appear confused and difficult to work towards.

Clear

Finally, the clarity of your vision is what will ultimately influence its success or failure. Although it may sound good if colleagues and students can repeat your vision to you, it is more important that they can discern the key points within the vision. What do you want to achieve and by when? Although your overarching vision may be longer than a quick slogan, it should be easy for anybody to remember what it is you want to achieve and by when.

Why you need to communicate your vision

Talking to people about your vision is arguably the most important thing you can do. Tell those in your team and senior leadership what you are thinking. Give them your big picture and then listen to the responses. This first step allows you to refine your vision with your team; not only does this allow them to buy-in to the vision but also ensures everybody believes it is achievable (Landsberg, 2002). The more you talk to people and listen to them, the clearer your vision will become.

After listening to the ideas of your team, senior leadership, teachers, students and parents, your vision will probably change. You may want to incorporate some of their thinking into your own. Collaborating with others and bringing in their ideas will help you make your vision stronger.

Once you have your vision and have worked through it with your team you can then use it as a clear reference point for any plans you put into place and decisions that you make (Eleftherios Boyatzis et al, 2007). When the school year is in full flow and decisions need to be made quickly it is always useful to have a vision to refer to. It allows you to think clearly about what you are doing and the impact it will have. Will decision that you make fit in with your vision for your year group? If not, what can you do differently?

Turning your vision into an ethos

Ethos is more difficult to manage as a head of year. It is something that takes hold over time but is heavily influenced by a clear vision. The ethos of your year group is simply the behaviours and ideals that characterise how your students engage with their studies, their teachers and their peers. Rather than something tangible it is more of a feeling about how students act while at school (Flores, 2018).

In order for your vision to become the ethos of your year group, a number of things will need to occur. First, you will need to make sure that everyone knows what the shared vision is and what the overall goals are within the vision statement. This is a really important moment because you are sharing with your team exactly what you want to achieve during your leadership.

Second, you need to make plans with your vision in mind. Your vision sets out the overarching goals and your plans (or strategies) should be designed to help you achieve those goals. Having everything you do focused on your vision will allow it to become embedded and, over time, this creates your ethos.

Whenever decisions are made, changes implemented and plans formulated, your vision should be the lens through which you view your decisions. There is no set formula for embedding an ethos within your year group; it requires consistency and relentlessly returning to your overall vision for your year group.

Case study

Jerome was a new head of year at a rural school that hadn't seen much staff change in the past decade. He took on a year group who had a well-established head of year in Year 7, and spent some time with no one clearly leading their group at the beginning of Year 8.

The school had its own vision statement proudly adorning the wall as you enter the school, which read: *'Our vision is to develop well rounded, confident and responsible individuals who aspire to achieve their full potential.'* Although Jerome believed this was a positive vision for a school, he felt that it could be the vision for any school and lacked the exclusivity of being specifically about his students.

Being new, Jerome didn't want to share his thoughts on the school's vision with the headteacher, but did want to create something more specific to his year group. He initially opted for: *'Our vision is to create a community of learners within our school who feel valued, respected and are encouraged to develop to their fullest potential.'* He started to discuss his vision with his tutor team, who expressed that they liked the overall message but would also like to see something about well-being in the vision as this was at the core of what they were trying to do.

Jerome agreed and settled on: *'Our vision is to create a community of learners within our school, maximising each student's sense of well-being, allowing them to develop to their fullest potential.'* Jerome then shared the final vision statement with his team and year group, securing the support of his colleagues in the process and ensuring everyone had bought in to this shared vision.

As Jerome went on to set out his plans for improving the year group, he routinely referred back to the shared vision statement he had agreed with his team, demonstrating to them exactly why they were performing certain actions within the plan.

Over time Jerome and his team continued to work towards their goals and routinely referred back to their vision as a shared ambition for the year group.

Summary

As you lead, you should be communicating your vision whenever you can. Staff and students look to their head of year to inspire them and keep them on the right track. The more you are enthusiastic and clear about where you are going, the more likely it will be that people follow your lead.

Don't underestimate the power of your shared vision. It is the rally call for your team and the central theme that should run through all of your strategic decision-making. Being able to refer back to a shared idea of what you want to achieve helps to keep everyone on board. You especially need to share your vision with parents and carers.

Your vision should be the lens through which you review the decisions you make regarding your year group as well as your future plans. When you apply this consistently it will, over time, create an ethos for your year group, that is the underlying characteristics that are visible to all who visit your school and interact with your students.

❖ Reflections

1. How will you develop your vision with key members of your team and students?

2. How will you ensure your vision is shared effectively?

3. What impact will your vision have on your team and your year group?

4. If someone was to visit your school, how would they explain the ethos of your year group?

5. How will what they say show your vision in action?

References

Buck, A (2017) *Leadership Matters.* Woodbridge: John Catt Educational.

Eleftherios Boyatzis, R, Rochford, K and Taylor, S (eds) (2007) *The Impact of Shared Vision on Leadership, Engagement, Organisational Citizenship and Coaching.* Lausanne: Frontiers.

Flores, L (2018) *Vision, Clarity, Support: A Leadership Crash Course on the 3 Pillars of Success.* Dar es Salaam: Mangrove Publishing.

Institute of Action Research for Community Health (2012) *Developing and Communicating a Vision.* [online] Available at: https://ctb.ku.edu/en/table-of-contents/leadership/leadership-functions/develop-and-communicate-vision/main (accessed 9 March 2020).

Landsberg, M (2002) *The Tools of Leadership: Vision, Inspiration, Momentum.* London: Profile Books.

16. MANAGING YOURSELF

What is self-management?

Much of your focus as a head of year is on how you will lead the students in your year group and your team of tutors. In order to undertake such a mammoth task, you need to be able to manage aspects of your own practice in order to be seen as a leader by others.

You must be able to demonstrate resilience and an ability to prioritise your own workload, develop yourself and your team, as well as work with multiple stakeholders. These skills don't simply appear. You must work to develop them within yourself and that requires self-management.

Developing your resilience

Without a doubt, there are times as a head of year when you will really need to dig deep and discover just how resilient you are. Indeed, developing your resilience is one thing that will help you to be a good leader (Shen and Moss, 2017). Resilience isn't about not feeling emotional pain or sadness but lies in your ability to adapt and make progress when facing adversity in the form of anxiety, trauma and stress.

As a head of year you will encounter many situations that you initially think are overwhelming or even deeply upsetting. A resilient head of year needs the thoughts, behaviour and actions to adapt at times like these and to support others in achieving the same.

In order to develop your own resilience, you need to first accept that change is a part of your work. That being said, you should always be hopeful that even in the face of change a positive outcome is possible. Keep all of the challenges you are facing in perspective; think long term about how you will move forward and avoid creating a larger issue.

The most important thing for you to consider is how you take care of yourself. In order to be resilient you must take part in activities that you enjoy, take care of your mind and body as often as you can and always have someone you can talk to at work who can support you and offer a different perspective on an issue, even if you can't share the precise details with them.

Prioritising workload

One thing that is true of every job within a school is the never-ending to-do list and competing priorities of the tasks you need to complete. Becoming a head of year adds to the list of things that require your attention and although it is likely you will be given additional non-teaching time to complete tasks, you must develop a system of prioritising your workload. One of the simplest tools I have found is the time management matrix (see Figure 16.1) developed by Covey where you categorise tasks by their importance and urgency (Covey, 2015).

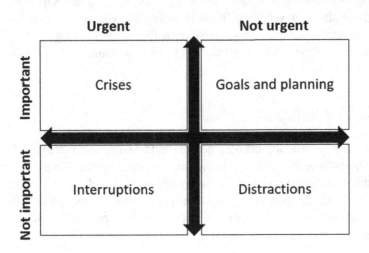

Figure 16.1 Covey's time management matrix

URGENT AND IMPORTANT TASKS

Tasks that are urgent and important require your immediate attention. The urgency indicates how soon you need to respond to an incident. As is often the case within schools, a number of issues can crop up after break or lunchtime which need to be dealt with straight away to avoid them escalating, such as a fight between two students or behaviour issues in a class that need your attendance to be resolved. Safeguarding issues almost always fall within this category and need to be referred to your safeguarding lead and any actions completed.

URGENT BUT NOT IMPORTANT TASKS

Not all tasks that need to be completed urgently are as important. Tasks in this quadrant might be low-level friendship issues that are causing problems within lessons or preparation work for a parental meeting which will help to support your discussions. It is sometimes wise to delegate these tasks to other members of your team, especially where urgency is key but you can't give the task your complete attention at that moment.

NOT URGENT BUT IMPORTANT TASKS

The not urgent but important tasks are often the ones a head of year would like to deal with most often. Much of your planning work surrounding how you will improve behaviour and attendance falls into this category; for example, reviewing strategies and devising new ways to motivate your students and look after their well-being. This work is essential if you are to be effective in your role as this is where most of your strategic work will reside. This category is most akin to the planning, preparation and assessment (PPA) time that you get for your teaching; without it your practice will suffer.

NOT URGENT AND NOT IMPORTANT TASKS

The final category is for tasks that are not urgent or important. There are times when some of these tasks will be inevitable within your working day; however, they should be discarded as much as possible as their lack of importance usually means they will have no discernible impact upon your year group. If you find you are spending more time focusing on such tasks you need to carefully review your workload and reprioritise. If much of what you are asked to do falls into this category, then you must discuss this with your line manager.

Balancing teaching with year leadership

Being a head of year requires balancing two roles: teacher and head of year (see Figure 16.2). First and foremost, you are a classroom teacher and you must remember this fact when going about your work as a head of year. When you are teaching, the students in front of you deserve 100 per cent of your energy and focus. However, your head of year role can seem much more important and urgent, often rightly so, and this is what creates such a tension.

Unlike a member of the senior leadership team, you are predominantly based in your classroom teaching lessons. Your role in leading a year group is in addition to this and you are given some additional time to complete this work. Due to the often immediate and sometimes serious nature of pastoral work, it can be easy to find yourself dedicating every second of your non-teaching time to your head of year role, to the detriment of your teaching practice.

You must always be mindful that your role as a head of year is reliant upon you performing in the classroom. You lead a team of teachers who also need support to balance their pastoral work as a tutor with their teaching commitments. Therefore, you need to be the master of balancing your two roles and always make sure you dedicate enough of your time to the core business of a school, educating children.

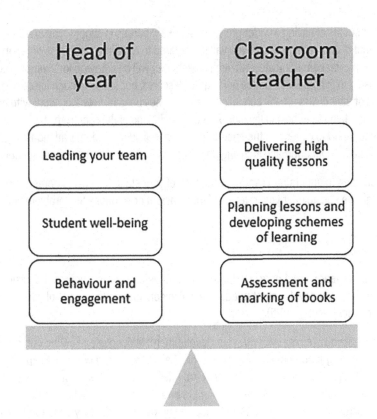

Figure 16.2 Balancing teaching and head of year responsibilities

Working with multiple stakeholders

Within a school there are a number of stakeholders with whom you will be expected to work at different points. There is a great deal of skill involved in being able to communicate with stakeholders such as students, families, senior leaders and local support organisations while also using these stakeholders to develop and improve your own work (Filho and Brandli, 2016).

Different stakeholders provide an invaluable 'other' view on your work. As the person driving the work with your year group you can often become so involved that you fail to recognise the bigger picture. Feedback from other stakeholders is an important part of developing your practice, seeking out new solutions and ultimately doing what is best for your students. Sadly, all too often, heads of year can be disheartened or apprehensive about the feedback of others with an involvement in their year group despite the potential it has to improve practice.

As well as the benefits of having a wider group of interested parties to support you in developing your practice and that of your team, at times you will be required to explain your actions or report back to stakeholders. How you communicate with each stakeholder will be different: for example, parents are seldom interested in average attendance or Progress 8 scores, but are very much interested in the minute details of their child's time at school such as how they behave, how they work with others and whether they are doing their best in lessons. At the opposite end of the spectrum, it would be wholly inappropriate to report to governors the finer details of an individual student's attendance issues. In these scenarios a broader approach focusing on averages across a cohort are more suitable.

Ultimately, you need to understand exactly what each of your stakeholders is interested in but also what they might be able to offer you in terms of fresh insight or solutions to a problem you are facing.

Developing yourself

What each head of year should prioritise for their own development is a personal decision. You should look at your own development needs while also considering the needs of your department and the wider school (McGill, 2015).

It is important that you are creative with your development. Making use of online communities such as Twitter or attending Teachmeet events in your local area are a good way to be exposed to bits of continuing professional development (CPD) that are relevant to your needs at a particular moment. While there are always courses on offer for teachers and heads of year looking to develop areas of practice, unfortunately not all schools will support you due to budgetary constraints, so taking ownership of your development is paramount.

One of the most effective ways of being able to develop your day-to-day practice is to reflect routinely on your work, what you have achieved and what you will do differently moving forward. There are many reflective models available to use and you should find a model that works well for you. An example is Gibbs' reflective cycle (Gibbs, 1988) shown in Figure 16.3.

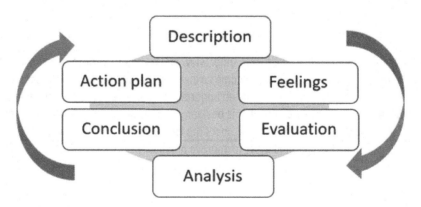

Figure 16.3 Gibbs' reflective cycle

KEY QUESTIONS FOR EACH SECTION OF THE REFLECTIVE CYCLE

Description

- What happened?
- What did you want to happen?
- When and where did it happen?
- What did you and other people do?

Feelings

- What were you feeling at this moment?
- How do you think others were feeling?
- What were you thinking during the situation?

Evaluation

- What worked well?
- What could have gone better?
- How did each person involved contribute positively or negatively?

Analysis

- Why did things go well?
- Why could some things have gone better?
- What do I need to know to understand the situation better?

Conclusion

- How could this situation have been improved?
- What skills do I need to develop in order to improve this situation?
- What else could I have done?

Action plan

- If I was in the same situation, what would I do differently?
- How will I develop the required skills?
- How can I ensure I act differently next time?

Look to the future

Despite your careful planning and preparation, it is always likely that change is just around the corner. You should always have an eye on the future, scanning the horizon for opportunities or concerns, and put a plan in place now. Try to avoid an urgent situation later on in the year by pre-empting issues now. For example, when the first murmurs of a new online craze start to surface, do some research for yourself and see what the potential pitfalls may be. More often than not it only takes a few weeks for a new craze to take hold and knowing what you are up against before it is too late is invaluable.

You should also keep your own aspirations high. Refining your working practices routinely will ultimately benefit your students and ensure you are always seeking new ways to develop yourself and your team. As you become more successful in your head of year role you may begin to think about what future roles may be available to you. This is a fantastic time to start looking at how you can impact upon the wider school in your current role and influencing other people doing the same role as you.

Case study

Anika was the head of Year 9 in a Greater London school. She was relatively new to her role and had found that her head of department was unhappy with the quality of her lessons. As a maths teacher Anika had always delivered what she believed to be good lessons but recently she had been turning up to lessons unprepared and sometimes late.

Anika was often on duty and would be dealing with pastoral issues which delayed her getting to lessons on time. One Thursday during the summer term, Anika was involved in resolving a friendship issue in the playground at lunchtime, and as the students were in her year group she took them to her office to hold a restorative conversation. As lunchtime drew to a close, the conversation between the students was in full flow and Anika didn't want to stop them despite having a Year 7 class to teach.

After arriving at her classroom to find her head of department settling the class, Anika spent the next five minutes setting up her lesson. By the time the lesson was underway the class had missed 20 minutes of a 60-minute lesson.

Despite the issue being one that could have been delegated to one of her pastoral managers, Anika tackled this incident herself, which had implications for the rest of her day. The balancing act between her teaching and head of year roles was clearly difficult to manage.

After this incident Anika sought out a head of year colleague for advice on how she could better manage her workload and prioritise what she needed to do every day. She was advised to use Covey's time management matrix and that she should delegate tasks that could be done by others while she is teaching. She was also advised to set time aside to reflect on issues she had faced each week and to plan how she could approach the same issues in the future. Over time it became clear to Anika that she didn't need to personally deal with every issue within Year 9, but she needed to work with other staff to give the students the best support possible while making sure she could teach consistently good lessons.

Summary

Your role often involves dealing with change and new scenarios. One of the key attributes of a good leader is therefore resilience (Britto, 2019). In order to manage your time you need to prioritise your work and ensure you focus as much time as possible on tasks that will bring about positive changes for your students and your team.

There are numerous stakeholders involved in your year group, all of whom can provide you with an insight into an incident or advice on how to develop what you are doing. With this in mind, it is important that you don't take the input of others as criticism; everybody wants what is best for the students. Recognise that as a head of year you are well placed to bring about change.

Personal reflection is a powerful tool in developing your practice, alongside any CPD opportunities that are available. Ultimately you need to take responsibility for your own development and through this you will bring about positive change for your year group.

❖ Reflections

1. How will you look after yourself to make sure you are resilient?
2. How will you manage your time between being a head of year and a teacher?
3. What strategies could you deploy to work with multiple stakeholders effectively?
4. How will you take control of your own self-development?
5. What plans do you have for your own practice in the future?

References

Britto, J (2019) *The Six Attributes of a Leadership Mindset.* London: Crown House Publishing.

Covey, S (2015) *First Things First.* Miami, FL: Mango Media Inc.

Filho, W and Brandli, L (2016) *Engaging Stakeholders in Education.* New York: Springer.

Gibbs, G (1988) *Learning By Doing: A Guide To Teaching and Learning Methods.* Oxford: Oxford Polytechnic.

McGill, R M (2015) *Te@cher Toolkit.* London: Bloomsbury Education.

Shen, C and Moss, S (2017) *Wrestling with Resilience: A Handbook for Developing Resilience and Mental Toughness.* Prahran: Black Knight Books.

17. MANAGING YOUR TEAM

Leading a pastoral team

Your team will undoubtedly consist of both teaching and non-teaching members of staff. It is often teaching staff who take on the role of tutors while there may also be an assigned pastoral manager, administrative staff or learning support staff that form part of your wider team. It is unlikely that you will have much input into who becomes part of your team and will probably not be responsible for their performance management (Nathan, 2011).

Despite these apparent difficulties you must lead your team for the benefit of your students. There is much that can be gained from having such a wide-ranging team who may not have otherwise found themselves working together. It isn't uncommon to have heads of faculty, heads of department, NQTs and full- and part-time teachers all in the one tutor team, with a full-time pastoral manager for support.

With such a mix of team members, there are a number of issues that might manifest and need to be dealt with swiftly and skilfully to ensure there are not long-term adverse impacts upon your students.

LACK OF TRAINING

Being a tutor is a skill but there is very little training available to support teams in developing this skill. This issue is compounded by the reality that those who need training are least likely to put themselves forward to attend. The solution is to frequently share examples of good practice within your team, demonstrate approaches to tackling issues and allow your tutors the time to observe more experienced colleagues.

LACK OF MOTIVATION

The reality for most tutors is that they joined teaching to share a love for their subject. Often being a tutor is viewed as a burden and the negativity caused by such team members can create real issues for you as a leader. You should share the benefits of providing strong pastoral care, highlighting how it will in fact enhance each student's ability to engage with their learning, help the tutor to develop meaningful relationships with students, and in turn draw students towards their subject.

ROLE TENSIONS

Due to the unique way tutor teams are built up, you can often end up managing staff who are actually more senior to you in the school hierarchy or middle leaders from other departments around the school. This can often make it difficult for people to accept you as the leader of your tutor team. It is useful to set out as early as possible what you expect of your tutor team, and follow up. The best way to tackle this is by demonstrating exactly why you are in your role; your passion and capability will eventually bring people on board. If it doesn't, there are always escalation points for bringing staff in line with your expectations.

INCONSISTENT OR POOR QUALITY PRACTICE

Working with a team of people who all have their own opinions on how things should be done can often lead to inconsistent practice across a year group or across a school. Similarly, some teachers are naturally better at this role than others. This is where you need to work on monitoring the work of your tutors, providing development opportunities and getting your team motivated to deliver their best work.

Motivating the team

First and foremost, your vision for the year group needs to be brought into play when you need to motivate your team. This shared idea of what you want to achieve should provide a rallying point and demonstrate the big picture of what your team is about. It provides a sense of purpose and states clearly what your values and those of the team should be.

In order to improve the motivation of your team you need to ensure they are clear on what their role is and, more importantly, how they can be great at it. Spending some time in your first meeting reviewing the role description of a tutor and then giving examples of what best practice looks like will go a long way to getting staff motivated and will provide a useful reference point for the future.

Your team need to be challenged by their work while still having autonomy within the role. Being too prescriptive can hinder some good work from taking place. However, it is right that where standards are not being met, some challenge is present to keep everyone working towards your vision (Buck, 2017).

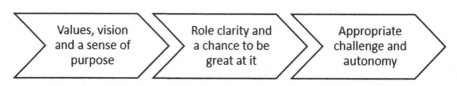

Motivating your team

Figure 17.1 Motivating your team, adapted from Buck (2017)

Setting expectations

If you are going to lead a team of professionals, they need to know exactly what is expected of them. I have already mentioned the need to review exactly what the role of the tutor is with your team as early as possible. It creates a 'base camp', a clear starting point from which you build up your expectations (Morrish, 2016).

The expectations you have of your team should be regularly reinforced. Over time this builds up and will become part of your overall team ethos where what you expect is immediately recognised by your team and others.

Whenever you set a task for your team you should also be clear about the outcome you are expecting. This ensures everybody has a clear understanding of what they need to do and the standard they need to reach. Having expectations of your team is in many ways similar to having high expectations of your students; quite often the higher your expectations, the more that is achieved.

Supporting the well-being of your team

The well-being of your team is just as important as the well-being of your students. The direct input you can have into the lives of your team is more limited, but there are things you can do to support them. For example, you do have control over aspects of their workload and exactly how some new initiatives or issues around the school are communicated with the team.

At times as a head of year you will be on the receiving end of a number of frustrated communications from parents, other teachers or senior leadership. When this happens, it can be tempting to go straight back to your team whom you had tasked with dealing with such issues and put more pressure on them by directing the same level of frustration at them. However, this achieves very little and does nothing to support the well-being of your team.

Nobody wants to do a job poorly and people on the whole are naturally motivated to try and improve what they do. Depending on the particular issue it may only require a gentle reminder to check the uniform of a tutor group, or a conversation to explain you have spoken to a parent and resolved an issue while demonstrating strategies to tackle the same issue in the future. In some cases it is proper to not share information where there is no real benefit to the team or the student. This requires a judgement call on your part as the leader of the team. If you have found yourself in a position where you have had to apologise for your team's work but are clear that there was no alternative, consider why you would want to share this message with your team. Is it to help avoid future incidents or is it simply to share the blame (Hesketh and Cooper, 2019)?

Finally, you have control over the to-do list of your tutors. One way you can support your team is to focus on key tasks that need to be completed in turn, rather than insisting a number of things are tackled at once. You also need to consider the deadlines that you set for your team. Are they manageable within the time they spend as a tutor each week alongside their other teaching commitments?

Leigh was the head of Year 7. He was given a new tutor team for September that included a number of middle leaders, an NQT and two classroom teachers on a full timetable. This initially presented Leigh with a number of challenges because although the middle leaders on his team were very skilled teachers, they were already very busy with their own leadership duties so might struggle with the pressure of being a Year 7 tutor. Likewise NQTs wouldn't normally have a tutor group and were on a reduced timetable. It would be unfair for Leigh to expect the same of them as of the other tutors.

At the first meeting with his new team, Leigh shared exactly what the role of a tutor involved and asked that each member of the team consider what barriers there might be to them being able to fulfil their role properly. Later in the week Leigh met with his tutors individually to discuss their thoughts on the role and looked at how he could overcome any issues. One of the classroom teachers was keen to develop this area of her work as she wanted to progress into pastoral leadership. The head of geography announced to Leigh that he felt being a tutor was a waste of time.

Leigh, aware of the time pressures many of his tutors would be facing, opted to focus on one key issue each week, initially starting with all students having the correct equipment for school. He asked the teacher who wanted to develop her pastoral work to devise a way of recording their monitoring checks. Leigh also spent time discussing why it was so important to have students prepared for their day of learning, emphasising the positive impact it could have on lessons, including geography.

By focusing on one task at a time Leigh was able to support his team and ensure that their well-being was considered. His work to provide opportunities to those who wanted to develop new skills while challenging the attitudes of other team members created consistency across each tutor group and over time the buy-in of the whole team increased.

Summary

As a pastoral leader you often don't have the same luxuries of hand-picking your team and line managing staff in the same way a head of department might. However, you can still have a great deal of influence over the working day of your team. Although it is possible to use the more formal management channels when members of your team don't seem to be engaging, it is often more productive to first try and boost their motivation for pastoral work and increase their buy-in.

You have the ability to add a great deal of pressure to the already pressurised workload of your teacher team members, so you must approach the handing down of tasks in a caring and considered way. The needs of your students are paramount, but if your staff don't have the time or the skills to complete the tasks you set, ultimately it is the students who will be disadvantaged.

❖ Reflections

1. How will you motivate a mixed group of professionals within your team?

2. How will you support the well-being of your team?

3. What will you do to address the lack of training that is often evident in the role of tutor?

4. How might you address poor performance from one of your tutors?

References

Buck, A (2017) *Leadership Matters.* Woodbridge: John Catt Educational.

Hesketh, I and Cooper, C (2019) *Wellbeing at Work: How to Design, Implement and Evaluate an Effective Strategy.* London: Kogan Page.

Morrish, A (2016) *The Art of Standing Out: School Transformation, To Greatness and Beyond.* Woodbridge: John Catt Educational.

Nathan, M (2011) *A Pastoral Leader's Handbook: Strategies for Success in the Secondary School.* London: Continuum.

18. MANAGING WORKLOAD

Look after yourself

It is important that you develop the skills necessary to manage your workload. It is necessary for you to adjust your working patterns so that you find a rhythm that allows you to get your job done while giving you time to spend on things outside of work. Where you fail to balance your work and life you can become stressed, leading to physical, mental and emotional ill health (Thomas, 2015).

Despite this need to manage your workload to safeguard your own well-being, a great deal of your work will be out of your control, such as your teaching timetable or urgent issues that need to be dealt with straight away. There is, however, a great deal of your work as both a teacher and a head of year that is within your control and by taking some key steps you can minimise the impact of the stresses on your health and well-being.

Your role is a demanding one and it is vital for your students. You are responsible for the well-being of the students within your year group, but how can you possibly do this if you can't look after yourself? It isn't sustainable for a head of year or any teacher to be working at the pace and depth than many do in the long term without there being consequences for those teachers (Holmes, 2019). Your well-being really matters.

The reality is that your workload has a huge impact upon your own well-being and the only way to ensure you can continue in your role is to get the workload in check. There is of course a caveat to this. At times in the school year you will experience times of intense workload as you work with students who don't readily conform to your timeline. To protect yourself you must acknowledge that this is a temporary situation and that you have the skills to tackle these situations and have colleagues who are available to support you.

Prioritise your work

Chapter 16 introduced you to Covey's time management matrix as a tool to help you prioritise your workload. There are many other ways you might chose to prioritise your workload. When faced with a new task you may find it useful to consider a number of key questions before deciding what, how and by whom the task should be completed (Allen, 2013):

- What is the task that needs to be completed and what is involved?
- How many people will be affected by this task?
- Does the task fit with my vision and goals?

- Is the job something I should be doing or is there someone else who should be completing it?
- What other times are available for me to complete the task if I don't do it now?
- Is the task time-sensitive?
- Can I delegate this task?
- How much time and effort will I have to give over to the task?

After considering these points you can either do the task immediately, plan a time in the future to complete the task or delegate it to a member of your team if it would be appropriate to do so. Regardless of your decision you must be realistic about what is being expected and don't bite off more than you can chew.

Remember you are a teacher too

Although the focus of this book is around being a head of year, you are also a teacher and your classroom practice needs to be a focus when it comes to tackling your workload. Your timetable will most likely not be changed to support your workload, so instead you should focus on key areas that can lead to time being used ineffectively.

- **Planning:** you can spend a lot of time working on individual lessons despite knowing that others within your department will be teaching the same lessons. Shared planning is a huge time-saver and helps you to 'tweak' lessons prior to teaching rather than planning them from scratch (Bubb and Earley, 2004).

- **Marking** can take up a great deal of time. Feedback for your students is important in order for them to make progress in your subject, but this doesn't mean that every piece of work must be marked by you. As a professional you need to use your judgement and deploy techniques such as whole class feedback, peer assessment and self-assessment to lighten the marking load while still ensuring your students receive clear feedback to drive progress.

Communicate clearly

It is easy to find yourself struggling with your workload, faced with a to-do list that is filled with urgent and important tasks. It is also true that unless you tell your line manager you are struggling to complete all of the work you have, they will not know there is an issue.

Sharing your workload concerns with your line manager doesn't necessarily lead to a quick fix but it allows an open and honest discussion about which tasks are completely necessary. Even if tasks cannot be removed from the to-do list, your line manager may be able to suggest different ways of approaching tasks or highlight things that you can delegate or ask administrative staff to support you with. The worst thing a head of year can do is take on every job that needs doing and burn themselves out. Your work is important for a whole year group of students and your team of staff; you can't do a good job if you allow yourself to become worn out.

Communication is also important when you give tasks to your team to complete. Some heads of year will avoid making any demands on their team that could lead to frustration, inaction and disconnection with your wider vision. This can happen because they want to avoid conflict or the possibility of someone saying no (Marshall, 2016). Your team need you to communicate your needs clearly to them. Linking these back to your vision whenever possible will give the tasks meaning and help to motivate your team.

Apply these principles to your team

One thing managers can be accused of is adding to the workload of their teams rather than helping to reduce it. If you are feeling overwhelmed it is likely that your team is also feeling the same.

It is useful to reflect upon your team's individual responsibilities and their collective obligations to assess which activities or tasks should be prioritised. Not all the tasks your team have to complete deserve the same importance and not everything has to be done immediately.

Setting priorities and realistic deadlines helps your team focus on what really matters and also helps to support their well-being. You should share the same workload tools you use with your team. Doing this enables them to feel a sense of ownership of their work and helps to prevent them from becoming stressed by their to-do list.

Case study

Ivan worked in a small school. He enjoyed the close community feel that the school had but it meant that tasks weren't shared around lots of people. He felt that although the workload was unmanageable he couldn't talk to anybody so instead he stayed late into the evening at school most days to complete the tasks he hadn't managed to complete during the working day.

After a number of weeks Ivan became unwell and was told by his partner that he needed to talk to the deputy headteacher who was his line manager to discuss all of the work he was trying to complete each day. Ivan had a day off work and although he should have been home resting, he felt guilty for not being in work and was still responding to emails from his bed.

When he returned to school the following day he sat with the deputy headteacher and explained that he had become ill because he was wearing himself down with work. Ivan outlined all of the tasks he was trying to complete each day while also teaching his classes on a 75 per cent timetable. The deputy head was shocked that Ivan was trying to complete so many tasks each day without any support and explored why he hadn't been distributing some of these tasks to his tutor team. Ivan explained that he felt guilty as everyone was under pressure so he wanted to protect his team. The deputy head understood Ivan's concerns but make it clear to Ivan that he needed to look after himself first otherwise he would not be able to do what was best for his students or his team.

Ivan also raised that he was spending a lot of time running reports from the school's systems in order to administer the behaviour and attendance policies. Without discussing his work with the other heads of year, Ivan hadn't realised that he could make use of administrative staff for the running of reports and the tutor team could hand out the individual report cards and make some phone calls to check on student attendance.

For Ivan, it took becoming completely worn out to realise that there were people who could support him in his work and that he didn't have to work late into the evening when everyone else had gone home. Ivan needed to understand that to provide the support his students and tutor team needed, he had to take better care of his own workload and well-being moving forward.

Summary

Your workload must remain in balance for the sake of your own well-being. You must acknowledge that schools are often slow to respond to workload issues and you must take ownership of your own to-do list. Prioritise your tasks and remove the pointless tasks while delegating those things that can be tackled by your team.

You simply cannot do every job that will come your way and you have a team there to support you. However, your team will also need your support in managing their own workload and you should apply the same prioritisation principles when allocating work to them.

Don't be afraid to make bold decisions for your team and remove tasks that you think are unnecessary. You should also be confident in discussing your needs with your line manager. Just as you try to support your team, they will support you too.

❖ Reflections

1. What are the issues that have the biggest impact upon your workload?

2. How will you ensure you prioritise tasks that you have to complete?

3. Which tasks will you discuss with your line manager? What difference will this make to your workload and well-being?

4. How can you refine your teaching practice to support in improving your workload?

5. How will you support your team in managing their own workloads?

References

Allen, D (2013) *How To Get Things Done.* New York: Penguin Random House.

Bubb, S and Earley, P (2004) *Managing Teacher Workload: Work-Life Balance and Wellbeing.* London: Paul Chapman Publishing.

Holmes, E (2019) *A Practical Guide to Teacher Wellbeing.* London: Sage.

Marshall, B (2016) *How to Communicate Your Needs At Work.* [online] Available at: https://flowchainsensei.wordpress.com/2016/08/24/how-to-communicate-your-needs-at-work/ (accessed 9 March 2020).

Thomas, W (2015) *Managing Workload Pocketbook.* Alresford: Teachers' Pocketbooks.

19. DEVELOPING LEADERS OF THE FUTURE

Working to make yourself redundant

It may seem odd, but in becoming a head of year, you should be looking for ways to make your year group and your tutor team self-sufficient. This means they should be able to resolve issues and go about their working week without your input. Should you accomplish this then you have achieved the ultimate goal in leading a year group and have taught your students and colleagues how to operate autonomously within the school environment.

In reality this isn't what is expected of a head of year, but it brings into focus how much you do on a daily basis to support your students and colleagues. You are relied upon to support them in a changing environment and ultimately you want your students to leave school able to be leaders themselves and for your team to be able to lead a year group one day too.

Before you can reach such a point, there is a great deal of self-reflection that must take place in order to understand how you lead others and how you can develop others in their own leadership journeys.

Leadership styles

Leadership styles are simply the characteristics or behaviours you display when directing, motivating, guiding and managing groups of people. There are many ways to look at leadership styles and there is a great deal of literature available to support you in this. However, the leadership styles first introduced by Lewin in 1939 provide a glimpse into how you may be operating as a head of year.

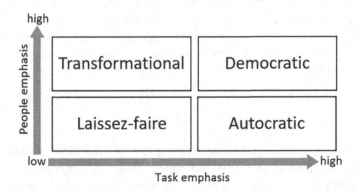

Figure 19.1 Leadership styles based on Lewin (1939)

AUTOCRATIC

Autocratic leaders make decisions without consulting their team members, even when this input would be useful. At times this style of leadership can be necessary; for example, when you need to make a decision quickly in order to respond to an urgent situation or in circumstances where getting the input of your team would not be necessary. However, autocratic leaders can be demoralising, which could lead to performance issues or even cause staff to feel undervalued and stressed.

DEMOCRATIC

Democratic leaders include their team members in the decision-making process, even if they ultimately make the final decision. This encourages creativity and increases buy-in from the team. This can also see the quality of work being done by a team improve. However, a democratic style can sometimes prevent quick changes from occurring and can leave people feeling frustrated when they don't agree with the decision.

LAISSEZ-FAIRE

Laissez-faire leaders give their team members a lot of freedom in how they do their work. They provide support with resources and advice if required but otherwise do not get involved. Although the autonomy can lead to high job satisfaction, it can be damaging if team members don't manage their time well, or if they don't have the knowledge, skills or self-motivation to do their work effectively.

TRANSFORMATIONAL

Transformational leaders aim to inspire their team members because they expect the best from everyone, and they hold themselves accountable for their own actions. They set clear goals, and have good conflict-resolution skills. This leads to high productivity and engagement. However, transformational leadership can at times create a chaotic working environment and make it difficult to present a united front.

NO FIXED STYLE

Although you will be drawn to one particular leadership style, you should recognise that different situations may require different approaches and moving between the leadership styles is common in effective leaders who are responding to a changing environment. It is likely that when faced with a stressful or challenging situation you will return to your most natural leadership position.

However, you must acknowledge the positive and negative attributes that go along with your leadership style and be aware of the impact this may have on your team.

Why understanding your leadership style is important

Everybody takes to leadership in a different way; some are more comfortable being the person who is accountable for any mistakes while others will go to great lengths to ensure they have controlled every element of the work being done by their teams (Morgan, 2020). You need to be clear on how you wish to lead your team and the potential drawbacks your leadership style may have on them.

By being aware of the potential issues, you are able to counteract some of the negative aspects of your preferred style and move more readily into another leadership style should the need arise. Being self-aware as a leader allows you to deal with a number of difficulties and manage the needs of your team at the same time. Most heads of year will tend to fall into the democratic leadership style when leading their team out of recognition that they are working with professional teachers. This helps to ensure your team feel valued and committed to their work.

When challenges come along it is easy to return to your default leadership position. Being aware of what that default position is will help you to understand why you take the actions you do in the face of difficulties and should prompt you to plan in advance how high-stakes decisions should be made within your team.

Mentoring your team

Mentoring is a way of bringing about a behavioural change within another person (Goldsmith, 2012). In this context you are wanting to bring about changes in your team members' practice that will not only improve the work they do with your students but also develop them as leaders.

When looking at how you can use mentoring to develop your team, it is helpful to decide on a key area of practice to work on. Once you have a focus, observe the member of staff completing this task, making use of this skill or delivering that tutor time session. Once you have done this, give them clear and actionable feedback, allow them time to build this into their practice and then observe them again (Bambrick-Santoyo, 2012). Mentoring focuses on having clear improvement points that need to be built into the team member's practice before you observe again and continue to find ways to improve their work.

Creating future pastoral leaders

The reality in most schools is that only a handful of teachers consider a pastoral leadership route for their career progression. Many see it as a difficult and unnecessary addition to the core business of educating students in their chosen programmes of study. One of your tasks as a current pastoral leader is to share with your colleagues exactly why a head of year role is such a positive career move. You need to radiate positive messages about how your job is one of the most rewarding within the school.

What is often overlooked by many within schools is that although pastoral leaders don't have a great deal of influence over the teaching and learning that goes on in the classrooms, they lay the foundations for this good work to happen in the first place. Without good pastoral care, where your students' most basic needs are looked after, some students would simply be unable to engage with their learning.

When students fall short of the expectations in a lesson, it often falls to pastoral leaders to remedy the situation to ensure the students can be in their next lesson ready to learn. I have said many times within this book that being a head of year is one of the best jobs within the education system. It is your job to make sure others get to experience the same privileged position in the future.

Case study

Isabel had been a head of year for six years. She had built up a strong and dedicated team of tutors who took care of much of the work that needed completing within the year group. Isabel found that more recently, her role was less about telling her tutors what needed to be done all of the time and more about responding to the changing needs of her year group and providing a space during her tutor meetings where plans could be formulated and put into place.

Within her team Isabel had a tutor, Tom, who was eager to progress in his career and become a head of year. Isabel knew that she would shortly be applying for promoted roles and was anxious that her year group and team would be led by someone she trusted to do a good job. Over a number of weeks Isabel began allowing Tom to have a greater input into the decision-making and planning of interventions for her year group. She observed Tom delivering some interventions focused on improving attendance and gave him some good feedback on how he should deliver some of the mindfulness elements of his sessions to support two very quiet students.

Over time Tom changed his sessions and was more aware of the students who had previously been going unnoticed. He was asked to share his intervention plans with the rest of the tutor team and to train other tutors in how they should be delivering their attendance interventions.

When Isabel came to leave the school Tom was appointed to replace her. This provided a greater sense of continuity for the team, and ensured the new head of year was familiar with the students and their issues.

THE HEAD OF YEAR'S HANDBOOK

Summary

Leadership is about more than simply giving instructions and getting your team to do as you have asked. In the case study, Isabel had built up a team over a number of years and had gained their trust and as a result they were performing well with less input from her. Isabel knew that if she was to be absent for a period of time or even move on to a new role, her year group and team would be able to continue as normal.

You should aim to achieve the same while recognising that this level of embedded practice will take time. When you are new to your role an autocratic leadership role may be more appropriate, moving to a democratic model once you have established how you want some aspects of your work to be done.

Being in a position where you can mentor your colleagues is a real privilege. It provides you with opportunities to develop your team in different ways, focusing on key elements of their practice that can benefit the work of the whole team in the long term and hopefully drive more people towards pastoral leadership roles within schools.

❖ Reflections

1. How would your year group get on if you were absent from school for a week?

2. How can you ensure there are people within your team who can lead in the future?

3. Which leadership style do you naturally fall in to and what impact does this have on your practice?

4. What are you going to do to help create future pastoral leaders within your school?

References

Bambrick-Santoyo, P (2012) *Leverage Leadership: A Practical Guide To Building Exceptional Schools.* San Francisco, CA: John Wiley and Sons.

Goldsmith, M (2012) *Coaching for Leadership: Writings on Leadership from the World's Greatest Coaches.* San Francisco, CA: John Wiley and Sons.

Lewin, K (1939) Patterns of Aggressive Behavior in Experimentally Created Social Climates. *The Journal of Social Psychology*, 10(1): 271-99.

Morgan, J (2020) *The Future Leader: 9 Skills and Mindsets To Succeed in the Next Decade.* San Francisco, CA: John Wiley and Sons.

INDEX

INDEX

Printed in the United States
by Baker & Taylor Publisher Services